"The ancient temptations Jesus experienced in the wilderness have morphed into toxic cultures of celebrity—and this is cause for great concern. Katelyn Beaty prophetically helps us to see the dangers compromising the church's witness in the world and ways we can live with greater integrity. This book is a great gift and should be required reading for all who love the church."

—**Rich Villodas**, pastor of New Life Fellowship;
author of *The Deeply Formed Life*

"The way of Jesus isn't usually found in brands, name recognition, or programs. It's found in relationships, humility, and servant leadership. In *Celebrities for Jesus*, Beaty beautifully reminds us that pastors and churches shouldn't try to compete with the world by looking like the world through programs, platforms, and numbers but instead should work toward resembling the life of Jesus by making 'little Christs.' *Celebrities for Jesus* is a much-needed book at this very moment in the church."

—**Chris Hennessey**, stay-at-home dad

"In this stupendously convicting and well-researched book, Beaty probes the soul of the celebrity pastor and, more hauntingly, examines how we the people help create such larger-than-life figures. With the inexorable transition to more online forms of discipleship in the digital age, *Celebrities for Jesus* provides a timely, sober reflection on the toxic culture that often arises when piety and popularity mix."

—**Jemar Tisby**, *New York Times* bestselling author of *The Color of Compromise* and *How to Fight Racism*

"The word 'celebrity' comes from Latin and its root means 'often repeated.' In this book, Beaty reveals how the stories of celebrities too often end the same way, even for those claiming to follow Jesus. With the tone of a trusted confidant, she shines a light on what happens behind the scenes of Christian celebrity culture. She illuminates the problem this presents to the church, while offering hints of ways we might change our current trajectory to prevent repeating history. It's a timely read."

—**D'Shan Berry**, follower of Jesus and lover of words

"We are in the midst of a reckoning on the role of celebrity within American evangelicalism. From her position of being inside the machine, Beaty brings two key elements to this compelling book. First, she brings knowledge and insights that will help anyone wanting to disentangle their faith from celebrity culture. But, even more than this, she offers an honest, humble self-examination that is a model many of us in the church need to follow."

—**Karen Swallow Prior**, professor, Southeastern Baptist Theological Seminary; author of *On Reading Well: Finding the Good Life through Great Books*

"This timely book offers the reader a close, revealing, and challenging look at celebrity Christianity. It doesn't point fingers but rather holds up an overdue mirror to American Christian pop culture. Beaty's journalism bona fides are on full display as she highlights familiar and maybe unfamiliar stories about large segments of American Christianity filled with unchecked power, manipulative charisma, and cultures of enablement. Her vulnerable self-reflection and theological survey are an added bonus that strengthens her credibility. This work contributes to a growing body of thoughtful commentary on church dysfunction with the hope of transformation."

—**Christina Edmondson**, leadership development consultant, Certified Cultural Intelligence facilitator, and cohost of the *Truth's Table* podcast

"We are living in an age where celebrities are not just the people we see on TV or the movies, but people who have grown a following on social media—and in Christian culture, the pulpit. *Celebrities for Jesus* perfectly captures how and why we continuously see popular Christian celebrity leaders fall from the high pedestals we put them on. Amid the scandals and heartbreak caused by trusted leaders, this book was a reminder of the power of proximity and true friendship that we Christians need the most."

—**Kellie Koch**, strategic communications professional

"With insight and empathy, Beaty diagnoses the broken patterns of leadership we see in the church. This book shows us the isolation and loneliness and abuse that can come from, and contribute to, these expectations of celebrity. But this book is no mere jeremiad. It points the way forward to renewed visions of power, account-ability, and humility."

—**Russell Moore**, chair of public theology, *Christianity Today*

"Media stardom is a relatively new phenomenon, but the corrosive-ness of power and authority is not. *Celebrities for Jesus* chronicles the abuses and scandals invited by the rise of eminent Christian personalities. It persuasively demonstrates that the embrace of celebrity culture is folly: whatever growth and outreach it achieves for the church comes at great personal and institutional costs."

—**James Havey**, attorney

"A wit once said a celebrity is a person famous for being famous, but the quip needs to be modified for American evangelical celebri-ties. For evangelicalism, a celebrity is someone who has formed, cultivated, and platformed a persona of themselves that attracts a following. In some cases, there is substance behind the persona; in many cases, there is not. In all cases, we need a demotion of the celebrity culture and the expansion of leaders who are followers of Jesus, the Jesus whose greatness came from the surrender of himself for the sake of others. I am so glad to see Beaty expose this serious problem in our churches. It will be a must-read for all those who want to lead."

—**Scot McKnight**, professor, Northern Seminary

CELEBRITIES
FOR JESUS

CELEBRITIES FOR JESUS

HOW PERSONAS, PLATFORMS, AND PROFITS ARE HURTING THE CHURCH

KATELYN BEATY

BrazosPress

a division of Baker Publishing Group
www.BrazosPress.com

© 2022 by Katelyn Beaty

Published by Brazos Press
a division of Baker Publishing Group
PO Box 6287, Grand Rapids, MI 49516-6287
www.brazospress.com

Printed in the United States of America

Library of Congress Cataloging-in-Publication Data
Names: Beaty, Katelyn, author.
Title: Celebrities for Jesus : how personas, platforms, and profits are hurting the church / Katelyn Beaty.
Description: Grand Rapids, Michigan : Brazos Press, a division of Baker Publishing Group, [2022] | Includes bibliographical references.
Identifiers: LCCN 2022003445 | ISBN 9781587435188 (cloth) | ISBN 9781493437030 (ebook) | ISBN 9781493437047 (pdf)
Subjects: LCSH: Christianity and culture. | Fame—Religious aspects—Christianity. | Evangelicalism.
Classification: LCC BR115.C8 B39275 2022 | DDC 261—dc23/eng/20220224
LC record available at https://lccn.loc.gov/2022003445

Baker Publishing Group publications use paper produced from sustainable forestry practices and post-consumer waste whenever possible.

22   23   24   25   26   27   28   7   6   5   4   3   2   1

To the number "who lived faithfully a hidden life, and rest in unvisited tombs"

Contents

PART 1

BIG THINGS FOR GOD

1

Social Power
without Proximity

When I accepted Jesus into my heart in 1998, in response to a gospel message at a youth rally at a local church, I had no idea what that event meant or the history it ushered me into. I just knew that I wanted to stand for Jesus—literally stand, as the speaker invited us to do. As a thirteen-year-old, I distinctly remember wondering what the boys in our youth group would think if I stood up from my seat, if they would call me a "dork" (the worst thing I could imagine at the time). But a stirring in my young, open spirit compelled me to stand no matter the cost. Riding home in the back seat of my parents' car that night, my heart felt warm, aglow with something new. It was like the strange warmth that John Wesley, the founder of Methodism, described experiencing after hearing a sermon on the book of Romans another world away.

The day after, I wrote in my journal, "I went to a Geoff Moore and the Distance concert on Saturday and it brought me a lot closer to God. . . . I think it saved me, or already made me realize I was saved. I'm glad I went."

I didn't know about John Wesley at the time, but it was fitting that my Christian conversion echoed his. Our family had attended United Methodist churches during my upbringing, as we moved every few years for my dad's military career. In 1996, we began attending a different kind of church: a "seeker sensitive" congregation in southwest Ohio. Mimicking popular megachurches like Willow Creek and Saddleback, it featured guitars during worship and simple sermons that often drew from pop culture. Our pastor wore open-toed sandals. His messages were simple, relevant, and positive. The approach was working: membership was growing, and the church was building a new worship center/gym featuring video screens on the walls. It was a UMC church, but nothing about our life together signaled to me that we were part of a tradition going back to Wesley. I had no idea we were part of an ecclesial institution with more than 12 million members in 32,000 churches across the globe.

Famous Christians were fixtures of my adolescence. After I came to Christ, I was introduced to musicians, speakers, pastors, and authors who would form my burgeoning faith, even though my only relationship to them was that I purchased their albums and books and heard their messages on a stage far away. This was the late 1990s and early 2000s, arguably the peak of evangelical youth culture. We learned we needed to stand apart from secularists who were forcing prayer out of public schools and filling young minds with *American Pie* and Britney Spears. Instead of questioning mainstream celebrity culture, though,

Christians had overall mimicked it. Secular culture had its celebrities, but so did we. DC Talk made edgy music videos that looked and sounded like Nirvana. Rebecca St. James was our Alanis Morissette, although all her angst seemed to be about retaining her sexual purity. Gospel artist Kirk Franklin had a crossover hit with "Stomp," with the lyrics "I can't explain it, I can't obtain it / Jesus your love is so, it's so amazing" blasting on the local top 40 radio station after Puff Daddy.

And the Newsboys drummer had a revolving drum set. *A revolving drum set!*

The strategy of swapping out secular celebrities for Christian ones was overt. At the 2000 Acquire the Fire conference, before thousands of teenagers packed into a stadium in Muncie, Indiana, Teen Mania founder Ron Luce told us to trade our profane CDs for their Christian alternatives. Like Blink-182? Listen to Five Iron Frenzy instead. Ditch the Mighty Mighty Bosstones for the W's. Sixpence None the Richer was okay, as long as we understood that "Kiss Me" was about Christ's love for the church. The lesson was that Christian youth could be cool and that the Contemporary Christian Music industry had produced the stars for us to emulate and identify with during our formative years.

As I grew up, I was also introduced to Christian authors pushing back against the rising tide of secularism coming for the country's politics and schools. At age twenty-one, Joshua Harris was thrust into the national limelight by making a stand for chastity and traditional courtship in his 1997 bestseller, *I Kissed Dating Goodbye*. Ravi Zacharias and Lee Strobel, famous international apologists, wrote scores of books making the case that Christianity was intellectually sound. We even had a Christian celebrity emerge from the 1999 Columbine shooting:

Cassie Bernall, who was alleged to have said yes when her killers asked if she believed in God. She and fellow victim Rachel Scott were hailed by Christian media and publishers as modern martyrs.

I didn't know it at the time, but these and other figures were part of a vast constellation of personalities who defined the evangelical movement in the late-modern West—much more so than did the vast expanse of church history, the creeds, or denominations. Later on, I'd learn that celebrity is a feature, not a bug, of the contemporary evangelical movement. However one traces the unwieldy history of evangelicalism—unwieldy precisely because of its decentralized nature—one finds a dynamic spiritual movement of Christians sharing the gospel using the tools at their disposal in a specific cultural context. Paul the apostle had shared the gospel using the tools of reason and philosophy in the marketplace of the Areopagus. He writes in 1 Corinthians, "I have become all things to all people so that by all possible means I might save some" (9:22). In a mass media culture driven by visual appeal, slick marketing, and personal branding, celebrity is just one more tool Christians have used to reach people for Christ.

Indeed, many Christians have used their fame, passion, and tech savvy for good kingdom purposes, sharing the gospel via mass media culture, whose global reach Paul could only have dreamed of. As far as we can tell (not knowing their inner lives), many famous Christians stand on these large platforms with integrity. To them, celebrity is one tool used to build the house of God—not the house itself. They're willing to part with their fame or prestige if it no longer serves primary kingdom purposes.

But other Christians have reached for the tool of celebrity and found that it isn't really a tool at all. It has more power over the user than the user has over it. It turns out to be a wild animal—cunning, slippery, and insidious. And that wild animal is now tearing up the house of God from the inside out.

Fame's Virtues

What are we talking about when we talk about celebrity? For a society fixated on status, image, and influence, you'd think we would have a better grasp of the celebrity dynamic. But the very nature of celebrity, especially in a digital era, is that it hides its power behind the illusion of intimacy. We need to look back to see how celebrity came to be at once ubiquitous and elusive.

Celebrity is a distinctly modern phenomenon fueled by mass media. Before that, we had fame, and we've always had it. Every age has featured individuals whose position, accomplishments, or political might have carried their name far beyond a single time and place. To be famous is to be known—or at least known *of*—by far more people than you can ever know. Fame almost always includes a differential of power.

Fame has often been an accident of birth, of bearing the right name or being born into the right family. Indeed, for much of history, fame has had more to do with your last name and your clan than with your accomplishments. Today, many of us follow with fascination the British royal family's inner dramas or scoff at the notoriety that comes simply from being born or marrying into the House of Windsor. Either way, the royal family captures how fame has often worked in times past. The queen is famous simply for being the queen—for who she is and the institutional and cultural power she represents, not really for her personality, talents, or Instagram game.

In a meritocracy like America (a meritocracy in theory, at least), fame often comes from what you do—skill, innovation, or accomplishment. Americans celebrate this kind of fame: the person of humble beginnings whose hard work and creativity have improved our lives or enriched our imaginations. Our national mythos rewards individuals for rising up from ordinary circumstances and wielding their talents and creativity to make our lives better. George Washington Carver and his peanuts. Walt Disney and his little whistling mouse. Steve Jobs and Steve Wozniak tinkering away in their garage. Americans instinctively believe that fame should be the reward for actually *doing* something. If someone is "famous for being famous," that is not a compliment.

Framed in a positive light, fame often arises from the desire to make something of our lives that will extend past our time on earth. Fame is connected to the innate human desire to create something that will last beyond ourselves, blessing or inspiring future generations. Creating culture is at the heart of bearing God's image; as humans, we can't help making culture. When we make culture well, in a way that benefits our neighbors or alleviates their suffering, sometimes we garner a kind of fame. We become known for being good neighbors in the public square. We become like the *tsaddiq*, a Hebrew word in Scripture meaning "the righteous"—people who are known in a community for personal integrity, generosity, and societal transformation.[1]

The right kind of fame arises from a life well lived, not a brand well cultivated. At its best, fame is a by-product of virtue, the effect rather than the goal of living a virtuous life. When we live as people who love well, serve sacrificially, pursue truth and justice, put others ahead of ourselves, and make the most of our time on earth, sometimes other people notice. Yet people of virtue, the *tsaddiq*, hold loosely any acclaim that might come their way. They share its power rather than hoard it. For virtuous people, fame—and any prestige and wealth that might come with it—is not the main thing. They are able to part with it as soon as it distracts from their primary goal of creating or leading well.

Fame is at its finest when it comes to those who are not seeking it.

Rosa Parks wasn't seeking fame when she refused to give up her seat to a white passenger on a bus in Montgomery, Alabama, in 1955. She was tired from a full day of work as an in-house seamstress at a department store. She was tired of being treated as a second-class citizen and second-class human under Jim Crow laws. She was tired of her black, female body being another locus for centuries of oppression and objectification against fellow Americans. For all of this, she was bone tired.

Parks's refusal to move for a white passenger on that December day gave fresh energy to the civil rights movement, inspiring the young minister Martin Luther King Jr. and other leaders to organize the Montgomery bus boycott, considered the first mass civil rights protest. She and others faced jail time and fines; her action could have cost her her life. There was a great risk involved in taking a stand by continuing to sit. Parks's act wasn't an open door to speaking engagements or book deals. She defended her and others' dignity and legal rights, and public attention and renown were the by-products of her virtue. Five decades later, when asked about her legacy, Parks said, "I would like to be remembered as a person who wanted to be free and wanted other people to be also free."[2]

The best famous people are the ones who seem to think about fame the least. Many of us can likely think of artists, teachers, government leaders, clergy, or business owners in our local communities who have gained renown because of how well they lead and serve. Of course, even on a national scale, many contemporary Christian leaders are household names presumably not because they set out to be, but because a mix of timing, talent, and the tools of media delivered their stories into our homes and hearts.

So, fame itself is not sinful. We shouldn't assume famous people, including famous Christians, are inherently shallow, power hungry, or hiding deep, dark secrets behind closed doors.

Scripture includes stories of God granting renown to certain figures to accomplish God's purposes throughout history. Esther is a striking example of a biblical figure who used fame and social power for godly purposes. She didn't start out famous—anything but. Hadassah/Esther was an orphan adopted by her cousin, Mordecai. As an Israelite teenager, she was chosen by Ahasuerus, king of Persia, to be his wife. She had little standing to resist the advances of the ruler of the largest empire of the day. After marrying the king, she could have settled into her new, glamorous life, enjoying the accoutrements of palace living and being the most beautiful young woman in all the land. Instead, she used her newfound proximity to power to plead for the powerless: to protect the lives of her Jewish people. Because of her pleading on their behalf, for the Jews "it was a time of happiness and joy, gladness and honor" (Esther 8:16). Esther was granted some fame and made good on it, becoming more renowned for saving the Jewish people than for being the king's trophy wife.

We might also think of the instructional role of the saints. In many church traditions, saints are revered beyond their lifetimes for singular lives of holiness, service, and sometimes martyr-dom. The Protestant and evangelical traditions have their own ways of remembering godly, prominent women and men. (If you doubt this, just visit the Billy Graham Museum in Wheaton, Illinois.) As a good Protestant, I think I'm supposed to say that all of us are saints—that because of Christ, all of us deserve to be honored equally. But it's simply the case that some of us "run the race marked out for us" with remarkable speed and grace; others of us—many of us—seem to limp to the finish line hobbling on one foot. It is right and good to honor Christians who run the race of faith well, because they inspire and instruct those of us who are still running.

Here's the trick: The vast majority of us will run our own races in ordinary, unglamorous ways, off the stage and off the screen. Almost all of us will live and die being known and loved (if we are lucky) by a small circle of friends and family—the people whose connection to us is deepest and most lasting because it was formed in daily, embodied, humble ways. For every famous saint, there are millions of ordinary ones. Ordinary people are the primary way God has worked in and through the world over the centuries.

More and more, though, it seems that a lot of us aren't content to be ordinary Christians.

Known for Well-Knownness

Celebrity is fame's shinier, slightly obnoxious cousin. It shows up to the family reunion in a Tesla, expecting a red-carpet roll-out. It will definitely share the whole thing on Instagram Live.

The word "celebrity" traces back to the Latin *celebritas*, meaning "multitude, fame." It comes from the Old French for "rite" or "ceremony," thus carrying a sacred, even religious connotation.[3] Simply put, a celebrity is someone who is widely celebrated. But celebrity is different from fame—and arguably more damaging—in at least two ways.

First, celebrity feeds on mass media. Celebrity is a uniquely modern phenomenon, spurred throughout the nineteenth and twentieth centuries, first through newspapers, then magazines, radio, film, television, the internet, and social media. Together, these media bring us into contact with "a vastly larger number of names, faces, and voices than at any earlier period or in any other country."[4] We feel connected to the names, faces, and voices on our screens—even though the connection is ultimately to a projection of a self rather than a true self. Mass media gives us the illusion of intimacy with famous people we follow and admire.

The primary functions of mass media are to entertain us and to get us to buy things. Thus, modern celebrities—including those in the church—feed the cycles of entertainment and material consumption. The tools of mass media, such as the screens in my church when I was growing up, are not neutral. As soon as an image of your pastor is projected onto screens across multiple sites, your church is borrowing from the worlds of entertainment and consumption, whether intentionally or not. The pastor on the screen is no longer just an expositor of the Word but someone we expect to entertain us or to sell us things. (Especially if the pastor has a book; more on that in chap. 5.)

Modern celebrities are often icons of success and wealth, and many are more than happy to have their names and faces co-opted to support our favorite brands. Michael Jordan might be the greatest basketball player of all time, but he is also one of the greatest company spokesmen, having earned an estimated $1.3 billion since first signing with Nike in 1984.[5] Nike's deal with Jordan wasn't just about selling shoes; it was also about selling us a vision of greatness. If you wear Air Jordans, maybe you'll play basketball like him too. Likewise with cosmetic companies, which sign deals with actresses to sell women the myth of eternal beauty. If Julianne Moore looks that great in ads for L'Oréal, maybe you'll look that great if only you buy this new antiaging skin cream.

A peculiar facet of celebrity is how manufactured it is—and it didn't start with Kim Kardashian. In his seminal work of 1962, historian Daniel Boorstin writes:

> The celebrity is a person who is known for his well-knownness. His qualities—or rather his lack of qualities—illustrate our peculiar problems. . . . He has been fabricated on purpose to satisfy our exaggerated expectations of human greatness. . . . He is made by all of us who willingly read about him, who like to see him on television, who buy recordings of his voice, and talk about him to our friends.[6]

A celebrity is known for their well-knownness—and we feed the problem. Boorstin highlights the artifice of modern celebrity: it is bought and sold through the channels of mass media as a good to be consumed. We don't always know *why* we're supposed to know who someone is, just that we should. It's similar to fame, but it doesn't require doing anything of particular importance, talent, or virtue. In this way, celebrity is often a shortcut to greatness.

It's an increasingly easy shortcut to take. Over the past decade, social media has democratized the celebrity pipeline, giving users the tools to project their image to untold followers, often with lucrative results. When I check Instagram, I am bombarded with content from "influencers," some with millions of followers. Social media influencers offer their followers "content" that is "relatable," yet almost certainly commissioned and created by professional photographers. They appear well lit and well dressed, stirring envy or aspiration. Even so, they assure us that their lives are just as normal and messy as ours. They offer candid snapshots into their daily lives, even though the actual content of their daily lives is lived off camera and can't in fact be truly known by anyone scrolling by. We seem to be okay with that, though; we're happy to consume the false intimacy.

The youngest generations are especially drawn to the idea of becoming "internet famous." After all, Justin Bieber was discovered on YouTube, and influencers with more than 1 million followers can make $100,000 per post for content paid for by brands.[7] In 2014, Yalda Uhls, a researcher at UCLA's Children's Digital Media Center, surveyed tweens (ages eight to twelve) about their values, compared with those of previous generations. She provided them with a list of seven values—community feeling, image, benevolence, fame, self-acceptance, financial success, and achievement. Of these, 40 percent of the tweens ranked fame as their top value.[8] Uhls found that "the biggest change occurred from 1997 to 2007, when YouTube, Facebook and Twitter exploded in popularity. . . . Their growth parallels the rise in narcissism and the drop in empathy among college students in the United States. . . . We don't think this is a coincidence."[9]

Reality TV and social media have removed many traditional barriers to achieving fame. Celebrity hopefuls think fame will allow them to feel desired and seen; live an elite, high-status lifestyle; and have a positive impact on their fans.[10] Celebrity is seen as meeting ultimate human desires for love, security, and purpose.

Second, celebrity turns icons into idols. Modern celebrities embody enduring worldly myths: We like them because we want to be like them. Celebrities embody what we celebrate. While most of us live ordinary lives, celebrities are always jetting off to a new premiere or tour, surrounded by wealthy and attractive people who boost their personal brand. As our bodies age and decay, celebrity bodies seem to retain physical strength and beauty. As most of us struggle financially, they seem to enjoy all that money can buy. As most of us influence only the people in our immediate circles, celebrities can shape attitudes, beliefs, and spending habits far beyond their circles. Beauty, wealth, influence, and immortality—these are enduring human desires projected onto celebrities and sold back to us as ultimate accounts of the good life.

Mass media acts to draw our attention toward particular people, telling us who's important to follow or know. Much to my chagrin, I know more factoids about my favorite actors, musicians, and comedians than I do about my flesh-and-blood neighbors. Mass media gives us the illusion of intimacy while drawing our attention away from the true intimacy available within a physical community, be it an apartment building, a book club, or a church.

It is right and good to look to virtuous people as *icons*. An icon is a representation of an image. We are all icons. A virtuous and holy person is someone who represents the image of God particularly well. They remind us of humans' original goodness and offer a glimpse of humans' destiny before sin ruined everything. Icons call forth the brilliance of the original image and make us want to image God more brilliantly. They are a conduit.

An idol, by contrast, images something other than God. Instead of being a conduit that draws our eyes up to the Lord of the universe, an idol replaces God as an object of devotion or embodies values and myths that compete with God as the original source of human joy and meaning: values like sex, money, and worldly power and ambition. True, most of us don't have literal shrines set up to worship our favorite actors, leaders, or influencers. But in the recesses of our hearts, our attention, and our wallets, our fascination with celebrities often takes up more of our imaginations than does our attention to God and our fellow image bearers.

I live in New York City, which means I occasionally see famous people on the street or the subway. Longtime New Yorkers tell me that the excitement wears off. Still, when I spot a celebrity, there's this odd emotional response. I feel excited when I see someone from the screen "in the flesh." (*They're right there! They ride the subway just like us!*) I kind of want to talk to them (I have been told to never do this) or just be near them. Depending on who it is, I want to thank them for their work or tell them how much they mean to me. There's a magnetic quality, as if by being around a famous person, I can absorb some of their glow.

There's a reason it's called "celebrity worship": our obsession with celebrities, or trying to be celebrities ourselves, betrays a spiritual hunger unique to late modernity. The decline of religion in the West means emptier churches. But the hunger for transcendence is as strong as ever. What humans of the past have found in traditional worship, fraternal organizations, and family and local community, we now seek in part by consuming images of people we don't and can't know.

Some theorists link celebrity worship to the decline of institutional religion over the past century. "A celebrity . . . is a 'personality' who can summon up primary psychological processes like identification, love, and adoration," write Deena Weinstein and Michael Weinstein. "Celebrity is methadone for the soul, produced by consumer capitalism to palliate unfulfilled psychological needs, social resentments, and spiritual discontent."[11]

It goes without saying that Christians can partake in celebrity worship too. Of course, we know better than to call it worship. Maybe we think of it as "honoring our heroes of the faith" or "following great men and women of God." We perceive that certain Christian leaders are particularly gifted or called to great kingdom purposes. And no doubt certain Christians are. The problem arises when our admiration becomes an ultimate allegiance, when we place superhuman expectations on a fellow image bearer that no actual image bearer was made to bear—certainly not alone and certainly not without deliberate limits on their own power and prestige.

There is a cost to our obsession with celebrity: what it does to fellow image bearers. Like all idols, it exacts a human price: loneliness and isolation; a strain on family life and intimate relationships; the pressure to keep up appearances when one's private life is crumbling, creating a divide in one's very self; the loss of privacy and solitude; and the temptation to escape the pressure with substance abuse and other addictions.

For the purposes of this book, I'd like to offer a definition of "celebrity" as *social power without proximity*. We put celebrities on pedestals, from which they influence, inspire, entertain, and exhort us. The power differential between us and them is, on one level, obvious. They are recognized in a crowd; most of us blend in. They are treated like very important people; we go about daily life as normies. Their work—whether in books, sermons, song lyrics, or script lines—is etched into the minds and hearts of millions; most of us are happy if just one person really hears and sees us. They get paid (often an exorbitant amount) to share their thoughts and talents, to influence; most of us do not.

Yet the power differential is on another level quite hidden, making it more insidious. Andy Crouch notes, "Celebrity combines the old distance of power with what seems like its exact opposite—extraordinary intimacy, or at least a bewitching simulation of intimacy." He continues,

> It is the power of the one-shot (the face filling the frame), the close mic (the voice dropped to a lover's whisper), the memoir (the disclosures that had never been discussed with the author's pastor, parents, or sometimes even lover or spouse, before they were published), the tweet, the selfie, the insta, the snap. All of it gives us the ability to seem to know someone—without in fact knowing much about them at all, since in the end we know only what they, and the systems of power that grow up around them, choose for us to know.[12]

We think we know our favorite ministry heads, worship leaders, authors, activists, and evangelists, because we follow them on social media or hear them preach from a stage or read their words on a page. But we are engaging with a presented, mediated self. And the absence of true knowledge, and true accountability, leaves abundant opportunity for their social power to be misused and abused. To have immense social power and little proximity is a spiritually dangerous place for any of us to be.

This is true not just for individuals but for entire movements. If recent headlines, evangelical consumerism, and my own up-bringing are any indication, the American church has overall mimicked celebrity culture rather than challenged it. We have too many institutions built around personalities—people with immense social power but little or no proximity. We're well past the point of thinking of celebrity as a neutral tool.

Fallen Leaders

On a dreary fall afternoon in 2014, I found myself in one of my favorite cities, on a trip with *Christianity Today* (*CT*). The magazine where I had worked as an editor for several years was preparing a cover story on women apologists, and I had been sent to Oxford, England, to profile one of them. As a college student, I had studied abroad in Oxford and ended that semester enchanted. I was grateful for another chance to walk its cobble-stone streets, passing under the Bridge of Sighs on my way to the King's Arms pub to end a long day of interviews with a pint.

But Oxford's charms couldn't quell the knot growing in my stomach as I prepared for another interview with the profile subject. She worked for an organization bearing the name of a famous apologist, and *CT* had received a disturbing tip about him in recent weeks. Specifically, we had heard from a source who wasn't ready to speak on record that the apologist had been seen at a hotel overseas with a woman who wasn't a family or staff member. Now I needed to ask the apologist if she could speak to his character and whether she had ever seen or heard anything that might lend credence to the tip.

After a long conversation about her scholarship, the time came for me to ask. A look of horror came over her face as I asked in as neutral a way as possible about this man's character, referencing the tip *CT* had received. She stated strongly that she had never seen or heard anything that would lead her to question the apologist's character or integrity. She suggested that, because he was such a public figure proclaiming the gospel in a hostile, secular climate, it was no surprise he had enemies—that rumors might spread from people who were trying to take him down and tarnish the reputation of the church.

She trusted him and I trusted her, and that day there was nothing more to ask. Honestly, I was relieved. I reported back to several editors at *CT* about what I heard, and the story lay dormant for years.

That is, until the truth about the beloved evangelist came to light, leaving his fans, his supporters, and the organization that bore his name in shock and grief.[13] We thought we knew him, but he had successfully evaded accountability and lived a double life, in no small part because of his global stature and fame and the trust we had placed in him from afar.

It wasn't the first time that *CT* had received a disturbing tip about a leading light of evangelicalism—a pastor, ministry leader, or entertainer who had been credibly accused of misconduct. As an independent, journalistic publication, we were responsible for digging into these tips and following the truth wherever it led. It sometimes seemed like a credible news source such as *CT* was one of the few institutions that could hold accountable these leaders who had apparently evaded accountability via other means. With every negative news story, *CT* got blowback: we were spreading gossip, destroying someone's reputation, or creating division in the body of Christ. But *CT* was compelled to report the truth out of *love* for the church, to expose "the fruitless deeds of darkness" (Eph. 5:11) and to seek some initial form of justice for the victims of those deeds.

Sometimes the tips we received went nowhere because sources weren't ready to speak on record. They were still enmeshed in the public figure's church or organization and were afraid of losing their jobs and social standing or facing other forms of retaliation. Other times the tips proved to be more complicated than presented, or they devolved into "he said, she said" narratives, with few ways to substantiate conflicting claims. But other times, such as in the case of the famous apologist, the tips we received proved to be horrendously true.

Over time, the more tips *CT* received, the more I wondered if the leading lights of evangelicalism were who they said they were. A casualty of working in journalism is cynicism: you start to hear troubling things, in part because people come to you, hoping that you'll look into an allegation. Over time, I started to wonder if the most famous Christian leaders—perhaps *because* they were so famous, existing in an echelon beyond most mortals—were truly people of deep Christian character. My journalistic eyes developed cataracts of suspicion.

Many of the fallen Christian leaders we reported on over the years had not started out as celebrities. They had started out in ministry by gaining a following for their accomplishments, creativity, or virtue—the previously explored healthy avenues for fame. They had wanted to serve their community or make a dramatic impact. Almost always, they had started out hoping to make more out of the name of Christ than their own.

But over time, it seemed, the fallen leaders managed to accrue immense social power without true proximity. They cultivated an image of spiritual importance while distancing themselves from embodied, in-person means of knowing and being known. Because they were so gifted or entrepreneurial or articulate, they had been allowed to evade normal accountability. Perhaps board members, colleagues, and donors had formally insisted on checks and balances, but the leaders were allowed to do and say things that others couldn't; they were just that important to the mission.

Over time, a chasm grew between who they were behind closed doors and who they were on stage or in their own sermons and anecdotes. They had started to believe their own hype. And adoring churchgoers, staff members, book publishers, and social media fans were at the ready to feed the hype, because they derived their *own* meaning and identity from a simulated connection to the celebrity Christian. These celebrities had amazing "platforms," and we, their fans and followers, had put them there.

The problem of celebrity in the church has now far eclipsed any temporary gains it might have offered along the way. But before diagnosing the multiple costs of celebrity power, we have to go back a bit, into recent history, to see how we got here and where we might have chosen another path.

2

The First Evangelical Celebrities

When I was a teenager—sometime after I had acquired the fire but before I had seen you at the pole—my parents invited me to hear Billy Graham preach. I vaguely knew who Graham was; I must have seen old preaching clips on TV, and some of his books lined our family bookshelves. I knew that earlier in his ministry he had befriended presidents and Hollywood actors, and that he was gentle and respectable compared with leaders of the religious right. He was well-liked even by people far outside the faith. He had earned the title "America's Pastor" for good reason.

Truthfully, I wish I had gone with my parents to the crusade. Instead, against their wishes, I stayed home to watch a movie with my atheist boyfriend. (By that time, I was bucking a straightlaced Christian image, and I quickly found that atheist boyfriends effectively rankled.) The rebellion didn't last long;

as a young adult starting out in my career, my first job was at *Christianity Today*, the magazine Graham helped found in 1956.

When Graham died at age ninety-nine in 2018 in his mountaintop home in North Carolina, it was a global media event. Glowing tributes poured out from Christians and non-Christians alike. Of course, Graham's life story was not without foibles and failures, many of which he later confessed. Over the years, he had been criticized for partnering with corrupt politicians, for marrying love of God and country during the Cold War, for insensitive comments about the LGBTQ and Jewish communities, and for his unwillingness to publicly support Martin Luther King Jr.'s dream of Beloved Community. Still, Graham carried himself with a humility uncommon in charismatic men who can draw millions into stadiums. He came to the end of his life without scandal or disgrace.

Like many of you, I'm sure, I have a complicated relationship with evangelicalism, the soil in which the seeds of my faith were planted. The term "evangelical" has been sullied by political alliances, by a central whiteness and resistance to racial justice, by a leadership culture that seems to reward bullyish men and silences women. Debates ensue about whether racism and misogyny are features or bugs of the movement. When people ask me if I'm an evangelical, I hesitate, chuckle awkwardly, then answer, "It's complicated." Even still, if an evangelical is defined as "anyone who likes Billy Graham," as historian George Marsden famously quipped,[1] I guess I'm in. I quite like Billy Graham.

But as virtuous as Graham was, he adopted and perpetuated some key weaknesses of the evangelical movement in the West. Even as he resisted celebrity, his approach to ministry helped fuel the dynamics of celebrity that now pervade evangelicalism. The movement he propelled throughout the twentieth century has seen celebrity power eclipse the power of institutions— centrally, the local church, which has always been God's plan A for taking the gospel to the ends of the earth.

To understand the outsize role of celebrity in American evangelicalism, we have to look back at the life of Graham— arguably the most famous evangelical of the past century—as well as other famous evangelists who inspired his approach.

Graham was born near Charlotte, North Carolina, in 1918, the oldest son of a dairy farmer. He was raised in a strict Calvinist family. But his genuine turn to Christ came at age sixteen. He came to faith in the same way he would later convert millions of others: through a series of revivals, featuring a charismatic evangelist named Mordecai Ham. Ham himself had been invited to preach through a group associated with Billy Sunday, a provocative former baseball player turned evangelist. Sunday had become a Christian through a colleague of Dwight L. Moody's.

So Graham's lineage traces back to Moody, the most famous evangelist the century prior. Graham joined a tradition of charismatic men who preached an individualistic gospel, used mass media to amplify their message, and aligned themselves with mainstream celebrities to lend cultural credence to their message.

Individuals First

For evangelicals, it's not enough to belong to a church, say the creeds, or even read the Bible. Being a Christian is not about "going through the motions" of a worship service or reading a traditional prayer. One must be "born again"—just as I was at that Geoff Moore and the Distance concert in 1998. The heart of evangelical faith is to make a personal, heartfelt decision for Christ, often in response to a powerful gospel message, and to invite others to do the same.

To be an evangelical, according to one classic definition, is to have an individual conversion experience and to verbally share the faith with others.[2] In this formula, individuals have a powerful experience with Christ that they try to inspire in other individuals. Such was the lineage that Graham stepped into, tracing back to Jonathan Edwards, John and Charles Wesley, and George Whitefield in the First Great Awakening, and to Charles Finney and Barton Stone in the Second Great Awakening. To be sure, these figureheads also belonged to institutions. They led churches, established missionary networks, and encouraged new Christians to join a local body of believers. But the first order of things was individuals coming to Christ, prompted by the preaching of a dynamic individual figure. The best way to change culture, they believed, was to change human hearts rather than to change institutions over time.

There would be no Billy Graham without Dwight L. Moody. Moody was born in Massachusetts to a poor bricklayer's family. He came to Christ at age eighteen after a colleague shared the gospel with him. Moody focused his evangelism in Chicago, among the city's poor and wealthy alike, through networks of businessmen as well as the YMCA. Historian Timothy Gloege notes that Moody had a distrust of church tradition and theology; he struggled to navigate "respectable middle-class Protestantism" and its emphasis on creeds, authority, and local church life.[3] He found more camaraderie among Chicago's Christian businessmen, who largely operated outside church structures. When Moody started the Illinois Street Church in Chicago, it was nondenominational and known as the Moody Church (the name it carries today).

When the church building burned in the Great Chicago Fire of 1871, Moody said God told him to focus on evangelism. To do so, Moody borrowed proven business principles to "sell" a down-to-earth, plain gospel to thousands gathered. He eschewed denominations and theological education. He believed anyone could know God by studying the Bible, absent the exegesis of pastors or scholars. In 1875, after returning from crusades in Europe, he was an international superstar—in no small part thanks to mass media coverage. Because of his outsize influence, at the end of the nineteenth century, "many Protestants from all denominations now understood conversion as a choice that inaugurated a personal relationship with God rather than a process whereby they entered a church community."[4]

Moody's successors mimicked his individualistic, anti-institutional impulse. J. Wilbur Chapman, a coworker of Moody's, began conducting his own revivals and hired as an assistant William Ashley "Billy" Sunday. Billy Sunday was a famous baseball player hired by the YMCA to leave the bat behind to join the revival circuit. He used punchy language, especially against liberals and evolutionists. Notably, Sunday was rarely tied to a church. He didn't see churchgoing as evidence of true faith. "Going to church doesn't make you a Christian any more than going to a garage makes you an automobile," he quipped.[5] He was ordained in 1903, but the road was a better venue for his preaching than the pulpit. He would run, slide, and jump across the stage, jumping up on chairs to express his outrage at the sins of liquor and dancing. He knew how to work a crowd with spectacle, and it worked, producing an estimated 300,000 converts.[6]

One of Sunday's converts was Mordecai Ham, a Kentucky-born fundamentalist who came from a long line of Baptist preachers. Ham was ordained but never actually led a church. Early in life, he had wanted to be a salesman, and he would later apply a salesman's charisma to saving souls. In 1934, a men's fellowship group—one named after Sunday—invited Ham to hold a series of revivals in Charlotte. It was at a tent meeting that Ham preached the gospel to a young Billy Graham. Night after night, Graham went to hear Ham, convicted of his sin and compelled by the message that God redeemed him, a sinner, through the cross of Christ.

Graham modeled his own ministry after these men. As a result, Graham derived his spiritual authority not from an institution but from his own charisma, passion, and communicative power. After graduating from Wheaton College, Graham took his first stint as a pastor in the Chicago suburbs. But it was also his last; he had global ambitions. He joined Youth for Christ International, touring the United States and much of Europe, capitalizing on a spiritual openness following World War II. From 1949 to 1952, he held nationally publicized crusades in Washington, Boston, Los Angeles, and other major cities, then hosted major revivals in London and New York. Wherever he went, he preached a gospel of individual heart change. And what people most remembered when they left a Graham crusade was how compelling this dynamic individual preacher was, not how compelling the local church is.

To be sure, Graham and the organization bearing his name partnered with churches in the cities they visited. The Billy Graham Evangelistic Association encouraged crusade attendees to join a church; Graham vowed never to publicly criticize congregations. But the daily warp and woof of Graham's global ministry happened beyond the purview of a local church or its leaders. And this was fitting, for in the evangelical lineage to which he belonged, it was an individual's powerful preaching that brought someone to Christ, not belonging to a church and its life together. The famous traveling preacher had replaced the local church as the link between Jesus and sinners.

My mom recently told me what it was like to see Graham preach in 2002, three years before Graham retired from his crusades. She and my dad went with friends from church to Paul Brown Stadium in Cincinnati. They had to catch a shuttle bus from the suburbs to the stadium—as did 50,000 other attendees. It was a powerful moment, she says: gospel singers Kirk Franklin, Nicole C. Mullen, and Michael W. Smith performed, as did a 4,000-person choir. "I remember the music and feeling of unity with so many other believers," said my mom. "I was caught up in the enormity of the event." And how could you not be? They were seeing America's Pastor preach in the twilight of his long career; it was rousing, as most revival events are.

But America's Pastor isn't quite the right title for Graham. A pastor is a shepherd of souls, and to shepherd a soul, you have to know that soul. From the stage and the screen, Graham—or any other Christian leader—can't really speak into others' lives with any specificity. Discipleship, as described in the New Testament, requires being part of a community, where you are known and *in fact know your spiritual leaders* too. But let's face it: Life in the local church and other Christian communities is messier and more frustrating than going to a crusade that gives you a spiritual high. Celebrity preachers and speakers are more dazzling than Pastor Jim in his pleated khakis. They won't ask you to tithe, ask about personal matters, or try to recruit you to volunteer at VBS. They are there to serve your personal needs for inspiration and encouragement.

Mass Media

A key feature of celebrity is the use of mass media—newspapers, radio, television, books, and the internet—to amplify the message and image of a famous person (see chap. 1). Mass media brings us into contact with more humans than any previous generation could have conceived. And mass media broadcasts a compelling message farther than at any other time in history. That was exciting for Graham and other evangelists of the nineteenth and twentieth centuries—the chance to save more souls justified the use of whatever tools were at their disposal.

The evangelists who inspired Graham harnessed the power of mass printing to create spectacle leading up to their revivals. Moody fostered ties with newspaper editors, creating a symbiotic relationship: the more the press covered his events, the more people attended, which would stir up more sensational headlines. Moody "publicly deplored any suggestion that men could make a revival, but he lived to see the day when his portraits sold briskly in the marketplace."[7] Ahead of one Boston revival, organizers used direct mail, billboards, and streetcar advertising to give the impression that "the revival is a big thing" and that "there had been nothing like it in Boston for a long time."[8] Journalists were given a box at the front of the auditorium before revivals, and the "media-generated spectacle took on a life of its own."[9]

Moody knew that this approach might draw attendees for the wrong reasons. People might come just to see the spectacle or to be entertained. But he thought this was a risk worth taking if a few men and women were converted along the way. The media coverage of Moody undoubtedly made him a celebrity—someone to know about, even if readers didn't always know the *why* behind the *who*.

Graham, for his part, enjoyed media attention without asking for it. Three weeks into his 1949 Los Angeles crusade, media mogul William Randolph Hearst gave editors across his chain of newspapers a two-word directive: "Puff Graham." The positive coverage brought an estimated 350,000 to the LA revival and made Graham a national celebrity at age thirty.[10] Not coincidentally, part of Graham's appeal was how attractive he was. Biographer Grant Wacker described him as the "All-American Male" with "a craggy face, blue eyes, square jaw, and wavy flaxen hair," and he noted that "for the better part of sixty years, virtually every newspaper article about Graham commented on his appearance."[11]

Graham may not have had a "face for radio," but he saw radio's capacity early on for reaching a lot of people. "Graham was an early adopter," Ed Stetzer, the Billy Graham Distinguished Chair of Church, Mission, and Evangelism at Wheaton College, told me in a phone interview. "He saw and harnessed the power of radio personally, and the crusades were widely broadcast on TV."[12] In 1950, Graham began the *Hour of Decision* TV broadcast on 150 ABC stations, and it quickly spread to 1,000. That decade, he began filming his crusades. Like Moody, his team would host press conferences before coming to a city to stir up attention. More than two million people came to hear Graham at his crusades at Madison Square Garden in 1957, the TV broadcasts of which garnered 1.5 million letters and 330,000 attested conversions.[13] His radio and television outreach continued through the decades, capitalizing on Americans' growing appetite for passive entertainment. He even joined an hour-long live chat on America Online (AOL) at age seventy-five.

Graham was a media pioneer, progressive and pragmatic in his embrace of new technology. He presciently saw the power of entertainment media to capture the hearts and minds of American consumers. And he embraced those tools to reach as many people as possible with a clear gospel message.

Living most of his life in the spotlight, Graham still came across as authentic and approachable. His charisma was undeniable, but he seemed down-to-earth. Graham was not about the glitz, and he did not seek out or flaunt a lavish lifestyle. Even so, mass media—especially the medium of TV—shapes the producer and the viewer alike to assume roles befitting the medium: namely, entertainer and consumer. On radio and television, preachers like Graham are entertainers whose message we receive and consume, often alone in our homes or cars, disconnected from embodied community.

The gospel comes to us in various forms: through the tool of language, whether heard or read; through actions and behaviors that glorify God; and most powerfully through the human life of Jesus and his preaching, healing, shared meals, sacrificial death, and resurrection. The gospel is always mediated. Yet if we take Christ as our model, we know the good news is shared most powerfully through relationship—through embodied love. God in Christ displayed his power by the radical "inefficiency" of close relationship with very few people during his earthly life. Jesus preached to gathered crowds, but he also regularly hid from the public eye. As Christians respond to the gospel, they form communities of love (the church) that speak the ultimate word of love to the world. It's worth repeating: the body of Christ has always been God's plan A for the world.

To be sure, evangelists in a mass media age have more "efficient" means of sharing the gospel than Jesus did. Graham noted this explicitly:

> Television is the most powerful tool of communication ever devised by man.
>
> Each of my primetime "specials" is now carried by nearly 300 stations across the U.S. and Canada, so that in a single telecast I preach to millions more than Christ did in his lifetime.[14]

If ministry success is measured by number of listeners, then it makes sense that Graham embraced TV and other media. Why preach only to one hundred when you have the tools to preach to millions?

But the medium doesn't just transmit a message; it changes the message. A medium designed for entertainment will transmute the gospel into a message of entertainment. Media theorist Neil Postman called Graham's rationale for using TV "gross technological naivete."[15] He notes in *Amusing Ourselves to Death* that when translated to TV, the gospel is stripped of everything that sets religious activity apart from other human activity, desacralizing it. Viewers can cook, pay their bills, or read the newspaper while spiritual messages play in the background, as long as the preacher-celebrity is engaging enough. Set alongside the nightly news and reality TV, the gospel becomes another form of passive entertainment.

Postman notes further that, when the gospel is televised, "the preacher is tops. God comes out as second banana. . . . Religious programs are filled with good cheer. They celebrate affluence. Their featured players become celebrities."[16] This was certainly true for Graham. By the 1970s, he was a regular guest on talk shows, including with Johnny Carson, Woody Allen, and Phil Donahue. He spoke in short, crisp sentences in a way that served an era of sound bites. According to Wacker, he was one of the few Americans who didn't need a mailing address beyond his name. If a fan wrote "Billy Graham" on an envelope, the postal service knew where to send it.[17] By the 1970s, he was known to many as "America's Pastor," enjoying insider access to the White House, even after the reputational damage caused by aligning himself with President Nixon. As his star rose, so did the evangelical movement he represented. Evangelicals defined themselves less by what they believed and more by who they liked and trusted. No one was higher on that list than Graham.

Famous Friends

In 1949, Stuart Hamblen was an actor and radio host who was fond of drinking, women, and singing about both. His wayward hobbies had gotten him into trouble. Then he met Graham in Beverly Hills, hosted Graham on his radio show, and attended one of Graham's crusades. After a few nights of internal wrestling, he called Graham at 4:30 a.m. to tell him he was ready to give his life to Christ.

It wasn't just a new start for Hamblen; it was a massive success for the crusades. Graham credited Hamblen's conversion—plus the "Puff Graham" support from Hearst—for bringing hordes to the Los Angeles crusades. Graham's other famous conversions during that time included track star Louis Zamperini and "Big Jim" Vaus, a wiretapper who had worked for mob bosses. These conversions boosted Graham's national profile and lent credibility to the Christian faith.

It wasn't the first time evangelists had forged ties with rich, powerful, and well-known people. Dwight L. Moody depended on well-connected businessmen to help fund his missions and international travels. As a former pro baseball player, Billy Sunday basically entered ministry as a celebrity, with ties to Woodrow Wilson and business tycoon John D. Rockefeller.

Because of his celebrity status, Graham found himself rubbing shoulders with actors, musicians, athletes, and royalty. Johnny Cash was a longtime friend who performed and spoke at many Graham crusades. Graham was friends with Martin Luther King Jr. and invited him to preach at a New York crusade in 1957. He provided spiritual counsel to every US president from Harry Truman to Barack Obama. He met with Muhammad Ali multiple times. He corresponded with Nelson Mandela during the South African leader's twenty-seven-year imprisonment. Queen Elizabeth II invited Graham to preach several times.

No doubt Graham enjoyed connections to such powerful people because of his personality and natural charisma. He was handsome, kind, and plainly likable. But he also forged such connections with famous people to establish the bona fides of the evangelical movement. Unlike their fundamentalist cousins, postwar evangelical leaders prided themselves on engaging rather than withdrawing from mainstream culture. Graham mimicked and embraced celebrity power. He showed that one could believe in biblical authority, the return of Jesus, and a literal hell, for example, and still hobnob with the rich and famous, including Cecil B. DeMille and Katharine Hepburn. He embodied evangelicals' desire for cultural respectability without having to water down their faith. Christians could watch him banter with Woody Allen and feel more confident in being both biblical and "relevant." Graham has a star on the Hollywood Walk of Fame. He shared the gospel with stars and, in doing so, became one himself.

Individuals over Institutions

In terms of people reached, Graham was arguably the greatest evangelist of all time, reaching an estimated 2.2 billion. His individualistic message, embrace of media, and ability to befriend powerful people bore much kingdom fruit. And, important for our purposes, he showed signs of spiritual health outside the spotlight in two key ways.

First, while Graham's preaching always emphasized individual heart change, he also invested in institutions that didn't depend on his gifts or charisma to succeed. Those organizations included Youth for Christ, the National Association of Evangelicals, Fuller Theological Seminary, the Lausanne Movement, *Christianity Today*, and the Billy Graham Evangelistic Association, among others that defined the postwar evangelical movement. Compared with Dwight L. Moody, Billy Sunday, and Mordecai Ham, Graham was firmly pro-church and pro-institution. He seemed to recognize the "radical idea . . . that the best things human beings do together are bigger and more lasting than any person who may occupy a temporary position of power."[18]

Healthy leaders understand that important work doesn't stop when they retire or die—that institutions are able to do much more over the course of time than one individual can do in one lifetime. Healthy leaders empower others to fulfill and carry out good works, understanding that the people around them serve the cause, not the top leader. It might be a cliché, but it's also biblical: healthy leaders understand that *we* is greater than *me*. In these ways, Graham was a healthy leader.

Second, Graham acknowledged his own celebrity early on and grappled with its unique temptations. Soon after he achieved success as a young, attractive evangelist, he safeguarded himself against the temptations of money, sex, and power that had felled other evangelists—most famously, Pentecostal preacher Aimee Semple McPherson.

The story goes like this: In 1948, in a hotel room in Modesto, California, Graham and three other men on his revival team agreed to never meet alone with a woman who was not their wife. Conversations about the resulting Modesto Manifesto tend to stop here: the Billy Graham Rule. When deployed by political leaders, the rule seems arcane and outdated for a world where women and men work together and thus need to meet one-on-one to talk about business matters. In Christian communities, the rule has been deployed in ways that make many Christian women feel objectified and sexualized. (I once showed up to a breakfast meeting with an older man, a Christian non-profit leader, only to find that we had a chaperone. It made me feel weird, as if my merely being a woman was a liability. I also wondered what he thought would happen over breakfast.) Sometimes the rule seems to be more about protecting male leaders from false accusations than about living with integrity—as if the real problem with meeting alone with women is that you might get canceled. Most crucially, the rule has kept women out of many rooms of power where their insights and accountability are sorely needed.

We tend to forget the rest of the Modesto Manifesto. In it, Graham and his team agreed to operate with financial transparency.

Graham's salary would be set by a board of directors, not determined by funds collected at crusades. Graham and other leaders bypassed the practice of some evangelists to pressure converts, in an emotional, vulnerable moment, to donate for the cause. They also agreed to work with local churches and pastors—to build up Christian institutions instead of setting themselves above or against them. Further, they committed to being honest about attendance figures, to resist reporting, for publicity's sake, greater numbers than they could prove.[19]

Graham saw with prescient wisdom how intoxicating it would be for leaders to believe they are so important that they can evade the accountability they need, even and perhaps especially when their work seems crucial for the kingdom. He saw that celebrity power's central lie is that an individual is important enough to be above the rules. He saw that celebrity so easily leads Christian leaders to use ministry to seek personal riches and thus defy the Bible's many warnings against greed and the love of money. He saw that celebrity causes many leaders to believe that they can go it alone—that their individual ministries and platforms are more important and central than the ordinary witness of local churches. And he saw that celebrity entices leaders to fudge the truth—whether attendance numbers or Facebook followers—to puff their ministry's importance.

The Modesto Manifesto's wisdom can be seen from the distance of today. The things that Graham and his colleagues tried to protect against have come true in many corners of the American church. As I've argued, Graham contributed to the problem of celebrity with an individualistic gospel, an embrace of mass media, and friendships with celebrities. But he also personally tried to guard against it by committing to institutions and communities where he could be known and seen as an actual human being—with weaknesses like the rest of us.

By contrast, many Christian leaders are swept up in the power of celebrity, with few tools to detect how it operates in their own souls and few safeguards for protecting against its outsize power in their churches and organizations. Part of the reason for this is simple: celebrity power in our day has far eclipsed the power of institutions, including the church.[20] In the two generations spanning Graham's public ministry, much of the Western world has seen the breakdown of the common forms and structures for organizing our shared social life. Institutions, notes political analyst Yuval Levin, are best understood as "the durable forms of our common life: They are the shapes and structures of what we do together."[21] From Congress to corporations to newspapers to the academy to religious communities, each institution performs an important societal task. And all of them are facing a crisis of trust at the deepest levels. Levin argues that most institutions today have failed to produce people of character, opening themselves up to corruption and other abuses of power. Today, institutions are more likely to serve as "platforms for performance and prominence" that leaders use to elevate their public image and their brand than as sites of collective good work and societal transformation.[22]

Describing American politics, Levin notes that political leaders use Congress—a quite important institution in our common life—"as a stage to elevate themselves, raise their profiles and perform for the cameras in the reality show of our unceasing culture war."[23] The boring but important work of legislation is capsized by outrage theater fueled by social media and an always-on news cycle.

Levin isn't much kinder to the church:

Look at many prominent establishments of American religion and you'll find institutions intended to change hearts and save souls frequently used instead as yet more stages for livid political theater—not so much forming those within as giving them an outlet.[24]

In other words, many of our religious institutions serve the individual leaders rather than the other way around. Churches become a platform from which pastors can expand their teaching influence far beyond the people in the pews, the very people whom pastors are called to serve. The work of religious nonprofits—such as the Billy Graham Evangelistic Association—is overshadowed by loud figureheads who use the organization to amplify their personal ideological agendas. And Christian book publishers and conference organizers tell Christian leaders that book sales or the conference circuit will be more influential and important than anything they do in their church or nonprofit. Institutions are too often platforms for self-expression rather than arenas of deep moral formation.

None of this is Graham's fault, of course. The evangelical movement to which he belonged was always going to favor charismatic individuals over institutions—especially individuals who could inspire dramatic heart change among riveted audience members. Evangelicalism—especially in the United States—was always going to place a premium on entrepreneurial individuals over and against dusty or "dead" institutions. That has resulted in dramatic, creative efforts to share the gospel and a willingness to try new methods and empower gifted individuals who might not otherwise fit neatly in denominational life or "churchly" culture. But it has also meant few gatekeepers, less accountability, and a greater potential for leaders to succeed on the basis of charisma, hustle, or a good game rather than a genuine desire to serve like Christ. We see that nowhere more clearly than in the megachurch movement, to which we turn next.

3

Megachurch, Megapastors

The local church is the hope of the world, and its future rests primarily in the hands of its leaders.

—Bill Hybels[1]

When he entered ministry, Bill Hybels really believed in the local church. In his book *Courageous Leadership*, he recounts when he first captured a vision of what a church could be. It was 1971, and he was a student at Trinity International University, outside Chicago. His New Testament professor, Gilbert Bilezikian, cast a vision of the Acts 2 church that was so compelling, Hybels marked that day as a clear before and after. He was captivated by a vision of believers whose life together reflected Christ's love for the world:

In that band of Christ-followers, believers loved each other with a radical kind of love. They took off their masks and shared their lives with one another. They laughed and cried and prayed and sang and served together in authentic Christian fellowship. . . . It was so bold, so creative, so dynamic that they [unbelievers] couldn't resist it.[2]

Hybels, from a family of West Michigan businessmen, soon abandoned his business major and began coleading a youth group. "Son City" used pop music, sketches, and relevant teaching to draw young people. Eventually there were more people attending the church's youth group than its Sunday services.

In 1975, Hybels left Son City to start a congregation that met at a movie theater in Palatine, Illinois. The church was designed in response to door-to-door surveys of what people said they didn't like about church. The goal was to create a Christian community that met individuals' felt needs. The approach worked: within the first three years, Willow Creek Community Church grew from 100 to 1,000, helmed by passionate leaders, with little infrastructure, and taking advantage of the chance to experiment with no denomination or board telling leaders to follow a formula. It must have been an exciting time, an echo of the Acts 2 vision that had inspired Hybels to enter ministry in the first place.

Of course, Willow Creek wasn't the first congregation to grow quickly or to use marketing techniques to draw spiritual seekers. Two decades prior, Robert Schuller (like Hybels, also raised Dutch Reformed) had gone door-to-door in Orange County, California, asking people why they didn't attend church. Soon after, Schuller began holding services at a drive-in movie theater where he'd broadcast positive, upbeat messages. His market-oriented ministry eventually launched the *Hour of Power* television broadcast and the impressive, glittering

Crystal Cathedral—what he once described as a "22-acre shopping center for Jesus Christ."[3] Hybels and another aspiring pastor, Rick Warren, explicitly drew from Schuller's model to start churches that would attract the spiritually curious by feeling less like churches and more like theaters, malls, and community centers all in one.

The megachurch, defined as a congregation with more than 2,000 members, is by one account a dynamic story of ministry success in a time of religious disaffiliation. Today there are about 1,750 megachurches across the United States, some with weekly attendance numbers of more than 30,000.[4] With an emphasis on *growth*—in buildings, budgets, and butts (seats in the pews)—the megachurch is a fitting American expression of the church. If traditional church is small and quaint, then megachurches shout that size matters. If traditional church is stuffy and boring, megachurches impress you with stylish architecture, hip worship leaders, and pop culture references. If traditional church emphasizes guilt, judgment, and sacrifice, megachurches inspire you with powerful messages of human potential backed by the Holy Spirit, who is ready to make your personal and professional dreams come true.

Indeed, since the model started taking off in the 1970s, some megachurches have matured past the growth-at-any-cost mindset, inviting attendees to deeper formation, turning consumers into disciples rooted in real community. Megachurches can be wonderful places for families looking for creative children's and youth programming. They can rally resources to serve their cities in times of crisis. Many have been on the front lines of tackling global poverty and providing clean water and education worldwide. And of course God can and will continue to use flawed church models for kingdom purposes.

But the megachurch has also altered our understanding of the pastor in powerful and concerning ways. Many megachurches turn their lead pastor into a celebrity and allow his individual power to eclipse the power of the institution. (The masculine pronoun is intentional here; as historian Kate Bowler notes, "Only a handful of women have ever led a megachurch in American history and their authority has been brittle."[5] Though there are exceptions, megachurches reflect the American evangelical preference for the top leader to be white and male.)

Beyond their size, their felt-needs approach, and emphasis on growth over depth, a defining feature of megachurches is how much attention revolves around the lead pastor—almost always "personally charismatic, exceptionally gifted men."[6] Compared with large Catholic and mainline churches, megachurches are the "product of one highly gifted spiritual leader," and the spirit and feel of the church reflect the vision and personality of the individual leader.[7] Naturally, the pastor brings on a plethora of staff and volunteers to carry out his vision for the church. But no one is mistaken about whose vision it is.

If the church "succeeds"—meaning it grows in buildings, budgets, and butts—then the church starts to believe that its success depends on the success of the pastor. The institution's identity becomes enmeshed with the pastor's; his public persona serves to draw fame and renown to the church. Having a celebrity pastor is seen as benefiting the church; all the better if you can get *actual* celebrities to start attending. Over time, a pernicious belief can set in: that the church wouldn't go on without the lead pastor at the helm. Almost as if God depends on the celebrity pastor to accomplish God's purposes. Almost as if the pastor is God himself.

Willow Creek was never the biggest megachurch. Its main campus, in the wealthy Chicago suburb of South Barrington, seats 7,200, which is modest in the megachurch panoply. In 2018, it reported 25,000 members across seven campuses. Joel Osteen's Lakewood Church, Andy Stanley's North Point Community Church, and Craig Groeschel's Life.Church boast far bigger weekly numbers. But Willow Creek was always the most influential, positioning itself as a model for churches hoping to mimic its growth. Starting in 1992, the Willow Creek Association (WCA) offered conferences, training, consulting, and other resources for churches that wanted to grow in the way it had in the 1980s and 1990s. By 2000, the WCA had more than 5,000 members, joined together not by doctrine but by methodology.[8] The WCA's *pièce de résistance* was the Global Leadership Summit, an annual conference featuring impressive speakers—CEOs, innovators, entrepreneurs, former presidents, even Bono. As of this writing, the summit (now rebranded as the Global Leadership Network) is broadcast in 123 countries and 60 languages, taking Willow Creek around the globe.[9]

Because Willow Creek has been the model for so many churches—and because of the latest, devastating chapter in its story—we need to examine the celebrity pastor thread at its core. To be sure, many other influential churches prop up their pastors as celebrities, confusing the church's identity with that of its most visible leader. Mars Hill Church rose and fell on the persona of Mark Driscoll, the brash founding pastor whose various controversies and abuses capsized the church in late 2014. Harvest Bible Chapel suffered a similar fate in 2019 when James MacDonald was fired for verbal abuse, bullying, and using church money to buy multiple homes, motorcycles, and hunting and fishing trips. And in 2020, Hillsong Church's global network faced a crisis when its NYC campus's lead pastor, Carl Lentz, was ousted for infidelity. These are only a few of the nationally visible stories; readers, I'm sure, will likely think of their own pastor fallout stories at the local level.

That said, the story of Willow Creek is worth recounting precisely because the church explicitly sold its celebrity pastor approach to other churches. That means its latest chapter could be replicated to disastrous effect.

In 2018, the *Chicago Tribune*, *Christianity Today*, and the *New York Times* published credible reports detailing sexual harassment allegations from several women against Hybels, dating back to the 1980s. At the time of this writing, Hybels, now retired, has continued to deny the allegations. An independent investigation commissioned by Willow Creek leaders in 2019 determined that the allegations are credible. In the aftermath, all the elders and several pastors resigned. Today, attendance and giving are down as the church tries to disassociate itself from the name of its most famous leader.

But the story of Willow Creek isn't just a story about one man's sexual temptations, as important as it is for any ministry leader to pursue integrity and accountability in that realm. The story of Willow Creek is shocking, but it's not unique. We see the noxious mix of charisma, anger, lack of accountability, secrecy, and VIP treatment on display in most other stories of moral failings of Christian leaders. Just as Willow Creek asked to be the model of megachurch success, it is sadly now the model of megachurch failure. And it started long before Hybels's abuses of power.

Seeker Sensitive

The campus of Willow Creek is both impressive and nondescript. Sitting on a ninety-acre wooded lot, the main building looks much like the corporate offices along Interstate 90 in the north suburbs of Chicago. Nothing about the architecture or style communicates "church," and that's the point. The parking lot is like an amusement park's, with row signs that help visitors remember where they parked. The first several rows are designated for drivers with disabilities and for first-time visitors.

Aimee, who grew up at Willow Creek and agreed to be interviewed for this book, remembers thinking the church was like Disneyland. When her parents arrived at Willow Creek in the early 1980s, the parking lot was gravel. "There was no steeple; it looked like a spaceship," she told me.[10] Growing up previously going to Catholic Mass, Aimee was struck by the building's contemporary feel and by how friendly everyone was. She remembers being surprised on her first visit when the children's ministry volunteer asked *her* what she thought of specific Bible stories.

Her mom thought the building was beautiful, and the family returned for several weeks, eventually becoming members. Her mother liked the music and ate up Hybels's sermons, which the family listened to on cassette tapes in the car. "Mom's Bible was filled with underlining," says Aimee. She recalls the Seeds Resource Center—the bookstore that sold books, Bible tags, and cassette tapes of CCM artists like Amy Grant and Sandi Patty. For people who grew up outside church, or whose experience of it was rote or impersonal, Willow Creek was a revelation. Hybels's teaching was approachable, easy to follow, and practical. Visitors learned that following Jesus would infuse their lives with joy and purpose.

Visitors who weren't interested in theological content found other reasons to come. For one, the music was top-notch, featuring professional singers and musicians performing songs that mimicked the day's radio hits. On the Sunday I visited, in 2021, a young, diverse team of eight to ten musicians took the stage, emerging from the haze of smoke against an edgy stage design. The lights went down as Sharon Irving—daughter of jazz musician Robert Irving III and a former contestant on *America's Got Talent*—led us through three worship songs. Visitors sang along to the lyrics projected on two large screens. Some raised their hands in praise. Others kept their hands in their pockets. No matter; visitors were free to engage in whatever way they felt comfortable.

Even visitors who didn't care about Sunday worship found plenty of other reasons to join Willow Creek, especially if they had kids. The weekend that I visited, the church was in the middle of summer programs. These included a pool party, a day camp, a young adults summer social, a women's book club, a blood drive, a men's conference, a backpack drive, and a performance starring kids from the ministry for children with special needs. For every way you can imagine slicing and dicing a church into target demographics, Willow Creek has a ministry catering to each one.

Laura Barringer began attending Willow Creek through its young adult ministry, Axis, which ran from 1996 to 2006. "It was vibrant connection and community," Barringer told me in a phone interview. "It was exciting. It was entertaining. . . . There was great music and drama, and our friends were there."[11] Attendees would meet up at the church's coffee shop beforehand, like the cast of *Friends* in the 1990s, when the idea of bringing your cappuccino into a worship service was novel. Axis met on Saturday nights and at its height boasted 2,000 weekly attendees. Axis folded in part because leaders felt it had created a separate church that didn't connect to the Sunday morning crowd. Even still, it spoke to what Willow Creek and similar churches do best: cater to attendees' felt needs in order to bring them into an exciting encounter with Jesus.

Casting Vision

Aimee's mother liked Bill Hybels's teaching. Her father, meanwhile, liked that Hybels was chaplain for the Chicago Bears. At that time, the Bears were enjoying new glory with coach Mike Ditka, winning the 1986 Super Bowl against the New England Patriots. A few Bears players, such as linebacker Mike Singletary, even attended Willow Creek. Aimee's father thought it was cool that NFL players were at his church and that he and other members could pray for them. "It was absolutely a way to get men to talk about God stuff," Aimee told me.

By that time, Willow Creek was on the cusp of national attention. With little formal theological education, Hybels and his team had grown the church to several thousand weekly attendees, with one thousand staff and volunteers needed to produce each weekly service.[12] Core to its success was Hybels's teaching, which was polished, clear, and often funny—something else Aimee's dad liked. Like Schuller, Graham, and Moody, Hybels knew how to arrest an audience with clear, powerful teaching that drove home a simple gospel message. "He's the best communicator I've ever heard," Barringer told me. "He's almost mesmerizing. His story examples, his manner . . . he can talk about leadership like no one I've ever heard."

"Mesmerizing" is an important word here; a person who has a way with words wields immense power over people. If that person is in a position of authority, setting forth a dynamic vision of the church for the twentieth century, they become all the more powerful. To sit under the authority of a dynamic speaker is, in a sense, to fall under a spell, to be persuaded and changed, sometimes in dramatic ways.

Hybels's power was in his preaching: "He's a jet-fuel drinking, high-octane, intense person, which comes through in his preaching to great effect," wrote the late preaching scholar Haddon Robinson. "That is Bill's charisma."[13] Most Sundays, Hybels spoke behind a plexiglass lectern on stage, tackling relevant topics with simple, compelling messages. After the service, he would descend to the right front corner of the stage, to an area known as the "bullpen." There, anyone from the church could come speak to him. Perched on the stage in an auditorium, Hybels might have appeared remote and inaccessible. He certainly didn't seem like a pastor who'd have the time to provide individual care. But the bullpen solved that problem, or at least gave the illusion of solving it. A few minutes with the wise, impressive visionary could change someone's life.

In *Courageous Leadership*, Hybels recalls attendees approaching the bullpen for prayer, healing, and financial advice. Hybels recounts a longtime member coming up one Sunday, poking him in the chest, and declaring, "Bill, they're gonna have to take me out of here in a box."[14] Hybels recounts this story to highlight that church leaders must cast a vision so compelling that lay leaders will give their lives to it. This man was telling Hybels, albeit in a colorful way, that he wanted to *die* at the church building. Hybels recounted this as a positive thing, as something other leaders should want to hear from those they lead.

Of course, sacrifice and devotion are part and parcel of the Christian life. Jesus said, "Whoever loses their life for me will find it" (Matt. 16:25). But when the call to sacrifice is set in a context like Willow Creek and other dynamic churches, it's not always clear whether members are being called to sacrifice for Christ or for the church and its programs. Loyalty to Christ and loyalty to the founding pastor's vision can get muddled. This is especially true if the pastor says that his own vision *is* Christ's—that God directly told him what the church should do next regarding its building, outreach, or finances. Elders or lay leaders who question those decisions are setting themselves up to question God. And who wants to look like they're questioning God? Especially when following the pastor's/God's vision has led to enormous growth, souls saved, lives changed, and communities transformed, and when other churches are looking to your church as the ultimate success story.

"Constant Applause"

By 1989, Willow Creek was certainly the success story. By then, says Nancy Beach, other churches were approaching the staff, asking how they did it. Beach, who described her experience at the church in a phone interview, had grown up attending Son City and was part of that early, exciting community that recalled Acts 2.[15] She and her husband stepped away from the church in the early 1980s, after it went through a period of multiple leaders' moral failures and ensuing conflict that Bill and his wife, Lynne, would later write about in their 1996 book, *Rediscovering Church*. At Hybels's urging, Beach came back in 1984 as programming director.

By 1990, she says, the celebrity dynamics—around Hybels and the church—were exploding. National media were starting to profile the church, and eventually the buzz went global. Hybels had published his first books, *Who You Are When No One's Looking* and *Too Busy Not to Pray*, in the late 1980s, establishing a national pastoral platform. In 1992, Hybels and staff launched the Willow Creek Association, a separate nonprofit to train and equip pastors and church leaders for dynamic growth. As long as it affirmed "a historic, orthodox understanding of biblical Christianity," any church could join for $249 a year. WCA members received workshops, books, video series, and newsletters. As a separate legal entity, the WCA had its own board of directors and a more traditional corporate function. There, Hybels interacted with executive leadership and staff as founder and CEO.[16]

By 1995, Hybels had also launched the Global Leadership Summit. Hybels would kick off the summit with an opening message and would come back on stage, appearing over the years alongside Colin Powell, Condoleezza Rice, Bono, Bill Clinton, Tony Blair, Craig Groeschel, and Steven Furtick. The summit boosted the church's profile as a "leader of leaders," a success story that could be replicated the world over.

"The leadership summit launched Bill into global celebrity," Barringer told me, noting its global broadcast and tens of thousands of annual attendees. "There was constant applause." But over the years, she started to become bothered by the focus on leadership. She remembers thinking that not everybody is called to be a leader, at least not in the CEO mold that the summit touted. From a biblical perspective, other gifts—such as encouragement, discernment, and hospitality—are just as important. But for Hybels, it seemed, the WCA and summit were his pride and joy, a place where his passion for organizational growth and vision could be fulfilled alongside highly competent corporate leaders. The Acts 2 vision of church that had launched his ministry career was surely still compelling. But running a business for other businesses that wanted to replicate *your* success proved especially intoxicating.

Behind Closed Doors

For all that could be said about Hybels's alleged behavior behind closed doors—and much would be said, starting in 2018—it's hard to grasp who Hybels *was* in the 1990s and 2000s. To be sure, he shared plenty of personal anecdotes in his thirty-plus books as well as in hundreds of sermons and talks. We knew about his wife and their marriage through books and seminars, and about their two children. We knew about the family home in Michigan and their love of being on the water. Hybels said he was committed to a healthy lifestyle after facing burnout earlier in ministry. In 1989, he said he informally reported to three male confidants, and in the coauthored marriage book *Fit to Be Tied*, he describes friends who were able to address dynamics within his marriage.[17]

Perhaps it's for the best that there's much we don't know about Hybels in private. But if celebrity is social power without proximity—and if only in true, intimate relationship behind closed doors are we really seen, known, and loved—then a warning sign for any lead pastor and their church is to be increasingly important and increasingly *unknown*.

For one thing, many Willow Creek members never saw Hybels, let alone spoke with him. Barringer remembers seeing Hybels in the lobby once and thinking, "Oh my gosh, it's Bill Hybels." The feeling was like seeing Steve Jobs in the halls of Apple headquarters or Oprah in the halls of Harpo Productions. Later, Barringer said, she stood in line to meet him. There were bodyguards. "I remember being very quickly dismissed," she said. "The sense was that he's very important and that there are a lot of people who want to meet him."

According to Barringer, as well as a staff member who worked in different roles from 2007 to 2017, Hybels didn't enter Willow Creek through the main doors. He had a private driveway and entrance. He had two offices, one of which was private, where Hybels would host other pastors and leaders. He wouldn't walk around the church without a security guard. And he spent much time away from the church altogether, using a private jet owned by the WCA to travel back and forth from Chicago to a beach home in Michigan. At some point he acquired a boat—it's unclear whether it was an official yacht or simply a large boat—and he would use it to host friends and ministry partners.

Setting aside the question of whether a pastor should own a yacht—an important question!—none of the above practices are, on their face, disqualifying. A case can be made that, given their visibility, pastors of large churches need special security measures. Or that they need spaces where they can have sensitive conversations. A case can also be made that these pastors deserve a compensation befitting their intense workload. How they spend their money—whether on very large boats or luxury sneakers or fishing gear—is up to them.

But taken together, requests for privacy and privileges can easily turn into demands for *secrecy*. Privacy honors the fact that every ministry leader needs elements of their life that are out of the spotlight. Even Jesus went away to be alone with God. Sabbath and rest are essential for every ministry leader, not least because your colleagues need to see that the ministry isn't dependent on you.

Secrecy, by contrast, creates a division between the private and public self, so that the private self can get away with things that the public self couldn't. Privacy says that if friends, family, or elders found out what the pastor did in private, they wouldn't be surprised or concerned. Secrecy, by contrast, makes sure no one can ever find out.

Indeed, as would later become pertinent, Hybels used a private email server. He said he did this because he had sensitive conversations with important people. "I'm in touch with thousands of pastors," he later explained. "A lot of people wanted to contact me about *very* private issues."[18] But no one could ever find out whether that was true. When allegations of sexual misconduct became public, more than 1,100 emails were discovered between Hybels and a woman. But no one could read them. They had been deleted or destroyed, as part of a "special arrangement" that Hybels enjoyed with the IT department.[19]

In theory, the church's board of elders would have been asking Hybels about these and other practices. In 1979, after the season of moral failings that had nearly capsized the fledgling church, it installed an elder board. The board was a group of volunteers who helped manage the church and to whom Hybels reported. In 2009, the elder board shifted to "policy governance," taking a more hands-off approach. There was also a board of directors and a management team, and, starting in 1992, a separate board and senior leadership team for the WCA.

On paper, all of these talented, kingdom-minded people would have held Hybels accountable. Indeed, a plurality of leadership and divisions of power are core to the New Testament vision of the church. Elders, bishops, and deacons are all prescribed as leaders with different overseeing functions. Different leaders at different levels bring a plurality of insights and gifts; they also, at their best, prevent top-heavy hierarchy, what might be called the "pastor and his staff" model, with one person at the top of a pyramid.[20]

But in a megachurch where the pastor is the visionary, founder, and CEO all in one, it's hard to know how much elders can really do. As Nancy Beach told me:

> Bill is also often the smartest person in the room. You look at who can speak truth to these larger-than-life leaders. . . . We talked a lot about accountability. It's not like that was a foreign concept or word to us. But I wondered, who could really go toe to toe with Bill? He's smart and good with words. . . . The board or the elders are holding these people accountable, but in reality, how does it work?

In other words, the eldership structure is not always a match for the strength of a leader's charisma. Indeed, an elder board can give the *appearance* of accountability while in practice rubber-stamping a leader's agenda. That is true for ineffective boards of businesses. But church boards carry an additional hurdle. "The pastor is in the role of spiritual father," noted Beach. "And now you're supposed to put on the hat of trying to hold a spiritual father accountable?" If Willow Creek's elder board comprised members who were highly devoted to the church, chances are they were also highly devoted to Hybels. It's easy to place someone on a pedestal who brought you to Christ or otherwise changed your life. It's hard to bring that person off the pedestal when your own faith and sense of purpose is tied up in their ongoing success.

It was later reported that the elder board failed to properly address the troubling allegations against Hybels, beginning in 2014, because he was *their* celebrity. The "Willow Creek Governance Review," published in April 2019, found that "the senior pastor was larger than life for many. Most board members gave deference to him. This made it difficult for some elders to challenge him in a meeting. . . . They felt like they were sitting in board meetings with a celebrity."[21]

The review also noted that the board's performance reviews went poorly because of Hybels's "defensive outbursts" and that "no elder would say that the senior pastor willingly placed himself under the authority of the board in a meaningful way."[22] The report notes a culture of fear, controlling behavior, and board capitulation as reasons why Hybels couldn't be stopped.

"Refracted Light"

"Bill is always right." That was one saying among Willow Creek leaders and staff. Over time, they had learned that disagreeing with Hybels wasn't worth it. Another saying, confirmed by the governance report: "the fear of Bill." This was in part what kept the elder board from standing up to him.

By many accounts, Hybels had anger problems. Anger is about control—needing it and the fear of losing it—and he certainly seemed to need it. His outbursts controlled other people's behavior. One former staff member I spoke with recalled sitting through worship run-throughs. "He would yell at people and make them cry" if he found something he didn't like, the former staffer told me. "He had full control, and that was true in every area of life at Willow Creek."

Another saying: If you ever made Bill angry, you had to bring him a bottle of wine. On one occasion, says the former staff member, a communications department employee included a typo in a document, which irritated Hybels. She was told by former pastor Heather Larson to go buy a bottle of wine for Hybels to make it up to him. He had a stash of nice wine bottles in his office.

If the megachurch model runs on celebrity pastors, it likely also runs on domineering and narcissistic ones. You probably have to be a touch self-important to think you can reinvent church and build a booming one from the ground up, to tell your congregation, "I've been all over the world, and this is the best church in the world," as Barringer claims Hybels would often say. The same qualities that drove him to create the most influential megachurch of the past fifty years are also the qualities that intimidated his colleagues and subordinates. That led him to pound his fist on the table when confronted with credible allegations of misconduct.

But it would be shortsighted to pin the problems of Willow Creek on one leader with anger issues. The stories of pastors' moral failures are of course stories about individual sins: anger, abuse of power, secrecy, giving in to temptation. But we'd be remiss not to take the story of Willow Creek as a chance to reflect on what *we* have done wrong. How have we contributed to the problem of celebrity pastors, often without realizing it?

In the end, the Willow Creek elder board was unable to hold Hybels accountable despite credible accounts of sexual misconduct spanning decades. For a while, they were *unwilling* to investigate those claims. Later, they greenlit one internal and two external investigations that were later deemed flawed. After the allegations were made public in spring 2018, the elder board, fellow pastors, and many lay members stood by Hybels as he called the allegations "flat-out lies" and said other leaders were colluding against him.[23] In subsequent "family meetings," top leaders echoed the narrative that Hybels's victims were lying or taking revenge on him. Only later did the elders and other top leaders apologize to the victims. All eventually resigned.

Celebrities wouldn't exist without us. They depend on our attention and adoration. We look to them to model who we want to become. Being around them makes us feel special and important. We feed their egos, and they feed ours. When a celebrity pastor invites us to join in their mission of changing the world for Jesus, we get excited that we've been selected for greatness. They fulfill what we've wanted to become: really important people for Jesus.

"People around the top leader get 'refracted light' from the central celebrity," said Beach, referring to a concept from clinical psychologist and trauma expert Diane Langberg. In other words, the professional and brand affiliation with the celebrity makes other people in the inner circle celebrities too. Beach acknowledges that she was given a platform as a leadership expert in part because of her connection to Willow Creek and Hybels. So does Barringer, whose husband once worked for the WCA. When she and her husband would travel overseas to WCA conferences, she says they were given special treatment because they were from Willow Creek.

Even regular Willow Creek attendees must have gotten some refracted light as well. Hybels was placed on a pedestal because he gave the Willow Creek community a deep sense of mission, purpose, and spiritual fulfillment. When he encouraged the church to reach its full potential because it's "the hope of the world," it must have been hard to resist that vision of being the hope of the world. By making Hybels important, the Willow Creek community became important too.

Aimee recently spoke with her father about the allegations against Hybels and his early retirement. Aimee was distraught over the allegations. The *New York Times* story detailing how Hybels repeatedly groped his former executive assistant was particularly upsetting. When Aimee's daughter asked her why she was crying, Aimee said, "A person I used to really respect made a really bad choice." To which her daughter answered, "Why does that keep happening?"

When I shared *Christianity Today*'s initial report on the allegations against Hybels on social media, I received a comment from an acquaintance. This person charged that *CT*'s reporting was skewed, that all they knew was that they were a Christian because of Hybels. The comment spoke to how painful it is to grapple with this question: How could someone who so positively ministered to you also be capable of hurting many others? Some deal with the cognitive dissonance by rejecting the news outright, as this acquaintance did: the allegations are false, the accusers are lying. Others come to see the leader as a mixed bag and go on to soberly reexamine their own experience with them in light of the fuller truth. Still others find it hard to separate the gospel from the charismatic leader, and they question the entire faith structure that the leader represented to them. Which is perhaps the most revealing and troubling element of creating churches centered on a celebrity pastor: if a person's faith in Christ is so centered on one powerful individual, when they fall, so do we.

PART 2

THREE TEMPTATIONS

4

Abusing Power

When Ravi Zacharias passed away in 2020, tributes poured out thanking the famous apologist for his ministry. Born in Chennai, India, Zacharias had founded and helmed the world's largest apologetics ministry, Ravi Zacharias International Ministries (RZIM), based in Alpharetta, Georgia. Claiming impressive scholarly credentials, he had written more than thirty books and traveled the globe, aiming to show the intellectual credibility of Christianity.

"One of my heroes of the faith is a man named Ravi Zacharias. . . . I'm so grateful for Ravi and his life and our friendship," said NFL player Tim Tebow.[1] "Ravi was a man of faith who could 'rightly handle the word of truth' like few others in our time & he was my friend," said Mike Pence, comparing him to Billy Graham and C. S. Lewis.[2] Franklin Graham, Jackie Hill Perry, and Paula Faris all posted on Instagram photos of themselves with the late apologist. It wasn't just celebrities honoring a late celebrity; there were people whose faith had been sharpened by Zacharias, giving thanks for a job assumedly well done. The Twitter hashtag #ThankYouRavi received 2.3 billion impressions.[3]

When I heard of his death, I'll admit I had a more mixed response. I remembered as a college student listening to Zacharias's lectures. At the time, I liked that he could go toe to toe with atheists and "elites" hostile to Christian faith. That made me feel that I, too, could be both smart and faithful. I knew how many people said they had come to Christ because of his messages.

But I also remembered my conversation with the apologist in England who worked for the ministry bearing his name. I thought about the tip that *Christianity Today* had received, that Ravi had been seen alone at a hotel overseas with a woman who was not an employee or family member. I also recalled a more recent, confusing allegation involving a Canadian woman who claimed that Zacharias had used his stature to sexually manipulate her. I wondered what had come of the tip *CT* received and this more recent story, and what the truth was in either case.

If you're reading this book, chances are you know the answer. Five months after Zacharias died, *CT* broke the story: Three women, employees at local spas co-owned by Zacharias, went on record saying he had exposed himself, groped them, and in one case urged them to have sex.[4] RZIM initially denied the allegations, then later hired a law firm to investigate the claims. In February 2021, RZIM released a report confirming the evidence that Zacharias had abused women at multiple day spas. The firm also found evidence of abuse in Thailand, India, and Malaysia. The report exonerated Lori Anne Thompson, the Canadian woman whom Zacharias had persuaded to send him sexual images, then had falsely accused of extortion. In fact, the investigation found, Zacharias had solicited hundreds of photos of women up until a few months before he passed away.[5]

Some of Zacharias's victims said his celebrity status made them hesitant to speak up. "You have this world-renowned evangelist who is being inappropriate, and I had no idea what to do," one woman said, noting that some of his books were sold at the spas. "He wasn't just the head of the company. He wasn't just a CEO. He was a Christian leader."[6]

Truthfully, I also thought about whether I, as a journalist and editor, had failed to seek the truth sooner. As an editor at *CT*, I had perhaps too easily assumed the best about Zacharias—not because I actually *knew* him or the contours of his life but because he appeared to be a glowing Christian leader whose ministry had helped a lot of people.

The story of Zacharias is disturbing on many levels. How could someone who preached the gospel publicly be capable of such harm behind closed doors? How could he have hidden his predatory behavior from so many colleagues and supporters? And how many people now question the credibility of his message because the man professing it fell so far? Sadly, the story isn't unique. Headlines in recent years have exposed how celebrity power can corrupt and shield abusers from accountability. Harvey Weinstein, Bill Cosby, Jeffrey Epstein, and many other famous men used their celebrity (and massive attendant wealth and prestige) to access, coerce, and silence. These celebrities often relied on other powerful people vouching for them or looking the other way in the face of disturbing allegations. Their sins were singular, but they were also systemic, enacted in a web of people who benefited from belonging to the celebrity's inner circle.

In chapter 2, we discussed evangelical celebrity and why the movement of Moody, Sunday, and Graham is uniquely prone to creating and defining itself by famous leaders, over and against institutions. In chapter 3, we examined the megachurch phenomenon and why large churches like Willow Creek so often feed the celebrity pastor problem. Both chapters aimed to provide historical context—how did the American church get here? In this chapter, we'll look at the costs of celebrity, and why and how celebrity power corrupts. It is a dark chapter, detailing the connection between celebrity and abuse and mistreatment of fellow image bearers. But if we're going to tame the wild animal of celebrity, we have to know what kind of animal we're dealing with. In order to heal the wounds of abuse, we have to examine just how deep the wounds are.

A Theology of Power

Money, sex, and power are the trinity of age-old temptations. But we have few resources for understanding what power is and how it operates. Personal finances and sexual integrity are regular topics in Christian books and sermons. By contrast, little is taught or written about power and its effects.[7]

Andy Crouch has written much to make up for this dearth. Like money and sex, power is not inherently evil. In fact, he writes, it is "a gift—the gift of a Giver who is the supreme model of power used to bless and serve." Crouch continues:

> Power is not given to benefit those who hold it. It is given for the flourishing of individuals, peoples, and the cosmos itself. Power's right use is especially important for the flourishing of the vulnerable, the members of the human family who most

need others to use power well to survive and thrive: the young, the aged, the sick, and the dispossessed.[8]

Power is the innate human ability to steward the world to glorify God and bless creation and fellow image bearers. God originally intended for all humans to exercise power as an extension of their bearing God's image. And, whether God intended it or simply because of how humans have organized societies and cultures since the beginning of time, some people have more power than others. Yet the mark of power rightly stewarded is that those with power enable everyone around them to flourish. People entrusted to their care thrive in material, spiritual, and relational ways, and are themselves empowered to steward their own power on others' behalf.

For those of us who have belonged to a community where power was stewarded well—where the people in charge were healthy, grounded, and humble—we know power can be a good thing. I experienced this at a Chicago-area church as a young adult. Our priest obviously held more power than us. He was formally trained to preach and lead in ways we were not. The power differential was obvious, symbolized by the robes and vestments he wore every week. Yet he was a shepherd entrusted with caring for the flock, and he held that high calling seriously and soberly. He stayed connected to Christ in spiritual disciplines. Church members could easily access him for prayer and direction. He was accountable to a vestry, a bishop, and other leaders besides. And he (and his wife) cared for me like a daughter. We were happy to grant him power because he stewarded it so well. We felt its good effects.

By contrast, if you have belonged to a community where power was stewarded poorly, you have seen the devastating effects. Perhaps you carry the devastation within you. When power becomes an idol—promising those with power that they can be like God apart from God—those in power seek not to bless but to dominate. They take what is not theirs, exploit, crush, defeat, gaslight, ridicule, and silence. In their presence, others feel *dis*empowered. And this is why power has such a bad rap, because doesn't this account of power just seem like the oldest story in the book?

This is the type of power Jesus warned against in Matthew 20: "You know that the rulers of the Gentiles lord it over them, and their high officials exercise authority over them" (v. 25). The operative word here is "over." Jesus is describing a power that seeks to rule *over* others rather than *for* others. Another translation of this verse says, "Their great ones are tyrants over them" (NRSV). Have you ever worked for a tyrant? They are harsh, unrestrained, and frankly scary. You feel disempowered rather than empowered because of the way they lead. And that's the point; they want you to quake, if only a bit, at their power over you.

This is not the power that Jesus's disciples are to seek. "Not so with you," Jesus says. "Instead, whoever wants to become great among you must be your servant, and whoever wants to be first must be your slave" (Matt. 20:26–27). And the disciples thought, *Sounds like kind of a bummer*. This wasn't quite the glorious life they imagined—or we imagine. If we want to be at the top, Jesus says, go lower. It's the opposite of what our idol-making hearts want.

Jesus's inversion of worldly power appears throughout his gospel teachings. He demonstrated those teachings through his death on the cross. People exercising godly power are willing to give it up in the ways Jesus did. They know that their power is provisional, deriving from God, and intended to be given away, not hoarded.

Here are some hallmarks of power rightly stewarded today, by people who seek to serve in the way of Jesus:

> The servant is the person who knows his or her spiritual poverty (Matt. 5:3) and exercises power under God's control (Matt. 5:5) to maintain right relationships. The servant leader apologizes for mistakes (Matt. 5:4), shows mercy when others fail (Matt. 5:7), makes peace when possible (Matt. 5:9), and endures unmerited criticism when attempting to serve God (Matt. 5:10) with integrity (Matt. 5:8). Jesus set the pattern in his own actions on our behalf (Matt. 20:28). We show ourselves to be Christ-followers by following his example.[9]

If our leaders hit even some of these marks—humility, mercy, peace, and integrity—we are grateful to have them in power. Ultimately, it is God's grace that allows any of us to steward power in the way Jesus did. I say this not to minimize our own responsibility to keep our power in check but to highlight how alluring and intoxicating power is. (If you don't believe me, go read *The Lord of the Rings*. I will refrain from recounting the plot in Elvish here. You're welcome.) The moment we think *we* wouldn't be enticed to abuse our power, we're in grave danger.

Few people go into ministry or leadership thinking they'll become tyrants, of course. It often starts with good motives. Someone with clear gifts and passion starts out wanting to leave a profound kingdom impact. They publicly embrace the concept of servant leadership. They sincerely submit to external accountability. They seek to bless others instead of dominate them. In the case of many leaders who ended up abusing their power, followers reflect back that the early days seemed pure.

They were drawn in by a vision of kingdom service, and the leader modeled it well.

Then at some point, maybe a leader feels what it's like to be treated like the most important person in a room. For a hush to fall over a crowd when they walk through the door. For people to hang on to their every word. It feels good. Perhaps their followers and supporters tell them they have special, indispensable gifts and that God has destined them and their ministry for kingdom greatness. That also feels good. If they are impressive communicators who can captivate a crowd, it's likely that they start getting invited to speak and teach all over the country. Their platform grows. It seems like God is expanding their reach. Book deals come their way. That, too, feels good. They can have influence, perhaps even on a national or international level. (More on the promises and pitfalls of Christian book publishing in chap. 5.)

At some point, maybe they start enjoying the accoutrements of success—nice dinners, first-class travel, time-shares, access to private VIP areas (whether in the nightclub or the country club), the chance to rub elbows with other important ministry leaders. And they start to believe that all of this isn't a gift but something they deserve. They are entitled to be treated like the most important person because clearly they *are*. They start treating people around them like they are not as important and lash out at anyone who might question their importance or restrain their power or spending.

And besides, look at all the ministry fruit.

A Way with Words

That is apparently how it started at Mars Hill Church. In 2021, the popular podcast *The Rise and Fall of Mars Hill* spotlighted the heartbreaking effects of toxic power at the Seattle megachurch—all the more heartbreaking, perhaps, because it didn't start that way.[10]

Wendy Alsup and her family joined the church in 2002. She was drawn by its vision to reach people who were skeptical of church, those on the outskirts of safe suburban culture. She thought Mark Driscoll's preaching was powerful, albeit inflected with a crass bravado. But it was working; people were accepting Christ, getting baptized, and becoming members. "We had so many people who were raised by atheist hippie parents," Alsup told me in a phone interview. "I longed to see the gospel moving forward. And it was, in this wild and crazy way."[11]

On the podcast, Alsup recounts a time Driscoll and his wife, Grace, let her stay at their home during a family crisis. Alsup received that gesture as a mark of true hospitality and pastoral care. To be sure, there were also early signs of anger, vulgarity, and blatant sexism. For years, Driscoll had posted anonymously in a church chat forum as "William Wallace II," going off on Mars Hill members for being weak or unmanly. Instead of shepherding the flock, he was essentially trolling them.[12] But Alsup told me in our interview that Driscoll had repented of the William Wallace phase, and she thought it seemed genuine.

Driscoll had the national media spotlight early in his ministry, as a self-admitted immature dude in his twenties. In 1997, after speaking at Leadership Network's annual conference, *Mother Jones* profiled him, and he was interviewed on NPR. The following year, he cofounded the Acts 29 church-planting network, in part because other pastors wanted to replicate Mars Hill's success. Starting out, Acts 29 revolved around Driscoll's "direct style of communication" and "charismatic personality." Driscoll's brash ways were "part of his magnetism."[13] The network structures were loose; as discussed in chapter 2, evangelicals are generally more energized by charismatic individuals than by creeds and denominational ties, and tend to center their ministries on (white, male) charismatic leaders. Acts 29 thus tended to attract and produce "young bucks" who modeled their preaching and persona after Driscoll. By 2006, Acts 29 had grown to 50 churches; by 2011, it was 410.[14]

Driscoll was a young star of the church-planting world. He shared stories from Mars Hill in his first books, published by Zondervan and Crossway. There was plenty of controversy over his comments—on women's roles, masturbation, "weak" men, pornography, stripping, Islam, liberals, and his wife's butt. Even still, he received the imprimatur of national ministries such as Desiring God and The Gospel Coalition. Despite his immaturity, he was embraced because he espoused correct Reformed doctrine and because Mars Hill was growing so quickly. Surely he would mature over time, with enough correction from seasoned pastors and theologians. Besides, any controversy seemed to amplify his celebrity, as if all attention was good attention. Part of the rationale was that the gospel itself was offensive, sure to stir backlash in a post-Christian culture. Fair enough, but not everything offensive is the gospel, and backlash is hardly evidence of godly leadership.

Back at Mars Hill, there were signs Driscoll was losing touch with the call to lead a church and shepherd the people therein. A former Mars Hill staff member who agreed to speak to me on the condition of anonymity said Driscoll said he wanted to become "America's Pastor," just like Billy Graham. "He loved the Billy Graham thing, because Graham was an evangelist, a Bible teacher—everyone knew who he was, and presidents talked to him." Like Graham, Driscoll had his sights set on a national platform.

"The fork in the road was the day Mark decided to broadcast himself in video," Alsup told me. By then, Mars Hill had multiple campuses, each with its own pastor. But instead of having the other pastors preach at their respective locations, Driscoll wanted his image and voice projected across all campuses as the main event. "They started centralizing [Mark's] teaching and Mark," said Alsup. "It wasn't about discipling and raising up other leaders. It was that he was the reason people were coming." Later, in an infamous 2012 meeting, Driscoll would declare to staff, "I am the brand."[15]

By then, almost everybody knew Driscoll got angry—like, a lot. He got hysterical at men he said were failing biblical manhood. He'd joke about "going Old Testament" on people who opposed him. But Mars Hill elders and other leaders knew the anger wasn't just a schtick. Driscoll's verbal wrath was being poured out on anyone who dared to disagree with his vision or curtail his authority. Celebrity power tells the celebrity that he can say anything, no matter how mean, tasteless, or perverse, and that others will shrug because the celebrity is too important or influential to correct.

Anger is a normal emotion, ranging in intensity from mild irritation to rage. We get angry when we perceive offense against God, ourselves, or others. Jesus got angry when he saw God's temple being defiled to feed greed and injustice (John 2:13–18). Jesus "made a whip out of cords, and drove all from the temple courts" (v. 15). Dude, the Son of God had a whip! (It's no coincidence that Driscoll latched on to Jesus's use of violence to highlight that "Jesus is not a pansy or a pacifist. He has a long wick, but the anger of his wrath is burning." This is no feminized, politically correct Savior.[16])

But Jesus's anger was righteous; ours, often, not so much. The New Testament names hostility, enmity, "fits of anger," dissensions, wrath, and malice as unacceptable for Christians. It says that a church leader "must not be quarrelsome but must be kind to everyone, able to teach, not resentful" (2 Tim. 2:24). Spiritual leaders should be gentle and self-controlled. But when your masculinity borrows more from John Wayne than Jesus, pastors like Driscoll often confuse bold leadership with being an SOB.[17]

Sinful anger often leads to verbal violence—lashing out at others so that they feel wounded or scared. In the case of Driscoll and other domineering leaders—such as former Harvest Bible Chapel pastor James MacDonald and financial guru Dave Ramsey—verbal violence is unleashed when they are challenged, corrected, or held accountable. (MacDonald was fired in 2019 after a church-led investigation found he was "insulting, belittling, and verbally abusing others."[18] And it was reported in 2021 that Ramsey has frequently berated staff for criticizing office culture to those outside their ranks.[19] He once allegedly pulled a "loaded pistol out of a gift bag to teach [employees] a lesson about gossip."[20]) Anger often reveals a clinging to worldly power. A person's anger reveals their need for control and their fear of losing it. (Again, not to return to *The Lord of the Rings*, but do you recall how Gollum acts around the ring?)

In October 2007, two Mars Hill elders were fired for raising objections to changes in the governance policy that consolidated power for Driscoll and a few top leaders. The next day, here's what Driscoll said at a church planters bootcamp:

76

There is a pile of dead bodies behind the Mars Hill bus . . . and
by God's grace there will be a mountain by the time we're done.
You either get on the bus or you get run over by the bus. Those
are the options. But the bus ain't gonna stop.[21]

This many years later, it's still shocking to hear a pastor talk
about running over people as a thing God will bless. The violence of the image is jarring and revealing. Driscoll might have
believed he was building unity, but "unity" forged by running
over those who question your decisions is just coercion. At
another bootcamp, Driscoll described a former elder as "a fart
in an elevator" and said, "If it weren't for Jesus I would be
violent"—as if he hadn't already enacted violence by his language and demeanor.[22]

By this point, people who had been hit by the Mars Hill bus
were talking online about their painful experiences. Driscoll
wasn't just a colorful bad-boy preacher; he was a bully. And
yet he still received praise and moral cover from The Gospel
Coalition, Desiring God, *Christianity Today*, and other national Christian organizations. The top leaders at Mars Hill
enabled his bullying—either because they benefited from proximity to his power or because they were afraid to become his
next target.

Over time, Alsup told me, Driscoll and his family were increasingly isolated from the church. He had special parking
spots and bodyguards, and he would come late to meetings
and leave early. Alsup, who had been deaconess of women's
theology and training since 2004, remembers trying to set up
a meeting with Driscoll. It would be at least a month before
he could fit her into his schedule. Not long after this meeting,
Alsup and her family left Mars Hill.

According to Alsup, Driscoll told Acts 29 staff that Alsup's family had left because "Wendy wore the pants in the family"—meaning, falsely, that she had usurped her husband's headship. "Well there you go—you just undermined my ability to be trusted," she told me in regard to Driscoll's comment. In complementarian circles where she had enjoyed chances to speak and write, Alsup said, it was hard to get her foot back in the door. Driscoll had once again used his untamed tongue not to bless but to hurt a sister in Christ.

Even still, Alsup told me, she benefited from catching the refracted light of Driscoll's celebrity; Driscoll had gotten her the contract for her first book, with Crossway. That was true for many in Driscoll's inner circle. Having the Mars Hill brand attached to your name could bring book deals, speaking gigs, and access to nationally known pastors and leaders. The rise and fall of Mars Hill is not just a story about one narcissistic bully whose temper (and publishing scandals—which we'll get to in chap. 5) finally caught up with him. It's also about the hundreds of people who baptized or excused his bullying, because they, too, were caught up in the appeal of celebrity power.

When Paul David Tripp, a famous pastor and author in his own right, resigned from the church's board of advisers eight months after joining it in 2013, he said, "This is without a doubt the most abusive, coercive ministry culture I've ever been involved with."[23] The operative word here is "culture," not "leader." Toxic celebrity power taints—and implicates—the whole institution.

Lavish Lifestyles

When news broke in 2020 that pastor Carl Lentz had been fired due to "leadership issues and breaches of trust, plus a recent revelation of moral failures," media outlets fixated on the "moral failures" part.[24] Lentz, among a crop of deeply V-necked megachurch pastors, led Hillsong NYC like a nightclub. The church attracted Selena Gomez, Chris Pratt and Katherine Schwarzenegger, the Kardashians, and Justin Bieber, to whom Lentz was like "a second father."[25] In late 2020, Lentz confessed to having an affair; later, Hillsong leaders said they found evidence of multiple affairs.[26]

News of Lentz's sexual misconduct was sad, if not surprising. It seemed Hillsong had chosen Lentz to be a celebrity among celebrities. The church featured a reserved VIP seating section, where pop stars and professional athletes were whisked away to get great views and meet Lentz backstage.[27] He didn't usually interact with "normal" attendees. Hillsong founder Brian Houston (who in 2021 was charged with allegedly covering up sexual abuse by his late father) admitted that he and other leaders didn't do enough to hold Lentz accountable, especially around issues with lying and narcissism preceding the infidelity.[28]

Hillsong also failed to stop Lentz from pursuing a lavish lifestyle; indeed, the megachurch seemed to encourage it as a missional goal to attract fancy people to the church. Former staff reported the use of prepaid cards that Lentz and other top leaders could use to buy whatever. The cards were loaded with members' and supporters' money and covered pricey meals, ATVs, and special gifts for other important visiting pastors—a practice that enjoys the spiritual euphemism "honoring." Meanwhile, the same staff reported being underpaid or going without pay, all while working overtime to keep the church running.[29]

Celebrity power breeds the lie that celebrity leaders deserve better, finer things because they are better, finer people—or because they are trying to reach people with the gospel who enjoy better, finer things. A common thread in the pitfalls of celebrity power is opulent wealth, pursued with ministry money, with supporters kept in the dark about how that money is used. Often, the people working around the clock to keep the ministry running are underpaid, which breaks the biblical command to pay workers fair wages (Jer. 22:13; Deut. 24:15).

Money is a fidgety topic for Americans, including American Christians. It's considered uncouth to talk about your salary at the dinner table. The more money someone has, the less comfortable they are talking about it, for wealth brings an uneasy shame in a highly inequitable society like ours.[30] For all that the Bible says about money—2,000-plus verses by one count—I can remember only a few sermons I've heard about it. Pastors might be afraid to talk about it for fear of offending members, perhaps especially members who give a lot to the church.

But money, like power, is not the problem in and of itself. Stewarded rightly, money can alleviate suffering, right generational wrongs, unleash creativity and beauty, educate the next generation, and make possible the life of the church.

I know personally the good that money can bring. I was born into a middle-class family featuring both generosity and good old-fashioned midwestern frugality. My parents have lived in the same one-story, three-bedroom ranch for nearly thirty years. They've never owned a luxury car. They rarely eat out. They financially support their church and local organizations. To be sure, by most of the world's standards, they are incredibly well-off. And as white Americans, they, and I, have benefited from the opportunity to create generational wealth that has been systematically denied to Americans of color. This is one reason, perhaps, why we don't talk about money; many of us who are privileged are ashamed of how we got it. That said, on an individual level, my parents are a model of stewarding money well—not perfectly, but faithfully. I wouldn't be where I am without their generosity.

The trick is, money is not a neutral tool, especially in a consumeristic, image-oriented society like ours. Economists, psychologists, and the biblical sages confirm that the more money you have, the more consuming it is—and the more complicated and stressful your life becomes.

The Bible warns against a love of money because it keeps us focused on earthly, not eternal, things. In the parable of the sower, Jesus says that the gospel will be choked out by "the cares of the world and the deceitfulness of riches and the desires for other things" (Mark 4:19). In the parable of the rich fool, he cautions followers, "Be on your guard against all kinds of greed; life does not consist in an abundance of possessions" (Luke 12:15). The apostle Paul warns that in the last days, "people will be lovers of themselves, lovers of money, boastful, proud, abusive" (2 Tim. 3:2).

Scripture makes a direct link between human greed and human suffering. The Old Testament is replete with commands not to exploit or mistreat the poor but to look out for their needs; the prophets decry those who amass wealth while ignoring the suffering of their neighbors. Scripture also warns against opulent wealth—showing off one's material possessions to impress others or inspire envy. Modesty is a biblical virtue, but not exclusively in the way evangelicals have taught it in recent decades. In 1 Timothy 2, Paul advises women to "dress modestly, with decency and propriety, adorning themselves, not with elaborate hairstyles or gold or pearls or expensive clothes" (v. 9). The point here is not that gold or pearls are inherently bad but that they signify opulence—lavish displays of wealth. Paul is telling early Christians not to draw attention to themselves with fancy things.

Perhaps it's because the American church has almost exclusively taught modesty as sexual purity that so many celebrity pastors miss the broader meaning. When Lentz and other celebrity pastors flaunt their luxury goods from the stage, they are anything but modest. On the popular Instagram account PreachersNSneakers, Ben Kirby has highlighted pastors who wear designer sneakers, watches, and other flashy clothing, showing photos of the pastors next to websites listing the price of their wares. Los Angeles pastor Chad Veach changed his Instagram name after Kirby shared a photo of him with a $1,980 purse and $795 track pants.[31] Pastors Rich Wilkerson Jr., Steven Furtick, and Judah Smith are fixtures on the account. So are prosperity gospel preachers, who have a theological rationale for flaunting their wealth: if you give to God, you, too, can wear Gucci.

According to Kirby, Lentz justified his luxury clothing by noting that it's simply what other New Yorkers wear. "I want to look like the people that we're trying to lead," he is quoted as saying.[32] The rationale is that rich people need Jesus too, and to gain credibility in wealthy circles, one needs to dress and act the part.

Fair enough; Jesus loved and befriended wealthy people, such as Zacchaeus and Joseph of Arimathea. But Jesus did not *become* wealthy in order to minister to them. He also loved and befriended many poor people. In fact, he had a special regard for people of lowly, humble means—people left out of the VIP rooms of their day.

Ministers of the gospel should, like Jesus, be free to minister to anyone regardless of their income. The problem with ministering to the 1 percent is that, once you're among the 1 percent, it can be hard to stay in touch with the 99. Wealth isolates. And when you yourself are wealthy, it's easy to spend most of your time with other people who are wealthy. In that bubble, you can start to think that fancy things—private jets, multiple homes, a closet full of designer clothing, in-home chefs and housekeepers, and $1,980 man purses—are both normal and totally what you need.

For ministry leaders, wealth can create its own rationales. What is initially a splurge becomes a necessity over time. For example, most of us likely scoff at the idea of a minister owning a private jet or regularly using one. But some high-profile leaders reason that, over time, it will cost less than flying first class, and besides, leaders can take meetings on a private plane. Of course, it should be noted that no one *has* to fly first class, and that ministers' time is no more valuable than anyone else's. Even still, if any of us had access to a private jet to scoot around the globe—or a yacht to host ministry partners, or multiple-million-dollar homes to enjoy family time or retirement, or a luxury man purse in which to store various accoutrements—we might very well justify it as both wise and good.

But Christian leaders should always ask whether their spending signals modesty or opulence—especially to those they are ministering to. The point here is not that private jets are always evil (although, on the whole, I'd argue their problems far outweigh their temporary conveniences). Or that nice meals, second homes, and expensive clothes are always and everywhere wrong. The point here is that all these things in our time signify lavish displays of wealth. To keep the worldly lure of money in check, Christian leaders should cultivate financial modesty—and ask others to hold them accountable to it.

The key to this accountability is transparency. Financial transparency means that staff, members, and stakeholders can easily access or request records that show how money is spent. Donors and tithers needn't see how their pastor or leader spends all their income. But they should be able to see what the income is, how it compares to other staff's income, and how it compares to the income of other pastors and leaders in similar fields.

In the United States, the IRS requires nonprofits to file an annual Form 990. This form includes information about "annual revenue, salaries of the highest-paid employees, names of board members and large contractors, and the amount of money the organization spends on administrative costs and fundraising."[33] The 990 ensures that ministries and nonprofits "are doing what they say they are doing."[34] That they are using donor funds for the purposes of the nonprofit, not to line the wallets of top leaders.

Because of the separation of church and state, American congregations aren't required to file 990s. More and more Christian nonprofits are taking advantage of this. In 2019, MinistryWatch reported that more ministries are switching their legal status from nonprofit to church—not because they are churches but so that they don't have to report to the IRS. Ministries that have made the switch include the Willow Creek Association, the Billy Graham Evangelistic Association, Cru (formerly Campus Crusade), and Ravi Zacharias International Ministries.[35] MinistryWatch leaders warn that this posture of secrecy rather than disclosure can easily be used to hide leaders' salaries and spending habits.

It is not within the purview of this book to dictate what churches should pay their pastors or what organizations should pay their leaders. I have my own opinions about what seems fair and what seems like too much money to pay an individual. Then again, I have never helmed a church or an organization. Nor have I experienced the immense responsibilities that would come with that kind of leadership. But for our purposes, what matters is that Christian leaders—and their organizations—be open and honest about their money. This means publicly reporting the leader's annual salary, keeping clear financial records, having a board or external oversight group such as the Evangelical Council for Financial Accountability review those records, having such a group regularly perform audits, and ensuring that charitable gifts and donations are going to the stated purpose.[36]

Power That Preys

If John Crist had been around in the 1990s, when I was a teenager, he likely would have been among the Christian celebrities I liked. Crist became one of the top 100 touring artists worldwide for his observations about evangelical culture. His social media channels poke fun at everything from contemporary worship to dating websites to moms who don't let their kids read Harry Potter. Crist rose to fame "precisely because he's what many young believers want to be: funny, smart, cool, relatable and vocal about his faith."[37] He had millions of online fans and crossover appeal, securing a Netflix special without uttering a single curse word.

That success came crashing down—or at least halted—when five women came forward in 2019 with claims of misconduct against Crist. Reported by *Charisma*, the claims included sexual relationships with married women, offering show tickets in exchange for sexual favors, and bragging about encounters with women after performing at churches, ministry events, and comedy clubs.[38] In response, Crist apologized for sinning "against God, against women and the people who I love the most."[39] He canceled his remaining tour dates. Eight months later, he reemerged to share that he had spent time at a treatment facility to address "sexual sin and addiction," before posting a video poking fun at cancel culture.[40]

Some of Crist's fans noted that the women who came forward willingly participated in what happened. In other words, no one had made them meet up with Crist, accept free tickets from him, or send him explicit texts or images. They were as complicit in sexual sin as he was. This may have been a story of one man's sexual addiction, but was it really a story about *abuse*?

Then again, listen to Kate (a pseudonym), the first woman interviewed by *Charisma*:

> I was blown away when John [Crist] agreed to do an interview with me for my senior project. . . . I was shaking and so nervous to be around someone I had idolized for months.[41]

Shortly after they met, Crist asked Kate to meet him alone outside his apartment. There, he gave her a water bottle full of alcohol and took her rollerblading. According to her, he told her that she was talented and that he could help her career. He later grabbed and propositioned her, after which she pushed him away, telling him she wanted a mentoring relationship, not a sexual one. As this was unfolding, Kate said, "I was truly blindsided by his celebrity status. There were a few moments I thought, 'Hey this is kind of weird,' but the same phrase kept playing through my head that stopped me from leaving: 'It's OK. He's a Christian. He won't do anything inappropriate.'"[42] Two years after the encounter with Crist, Kate said she struggles with "what it means to be Christian after being so disgustingly let down by a role model I considered a man of God."[43]

Crist was able to act as he did for two reasons: He was a celebrity who seemed to have a blinding effect on some fans. And he was a *Christian* celebrity. Because someone has a Christian platform and creates Christian content, fans assume he is a mature disciple of Christ and will treat them with integrity and respect.

Of course, abuse happens in small and large churches, in every denomination, across barriers of race, class, age, and creed. The #ChurchToo movement highlights that abuse can happen whenever a person, celebrity or not, wields power over another person. The violation of another person's body for sexual gratification is one of the most destructive expressions of power gone bad. Many survivors carry emotional, psychological, and spiritual wounds decades after they've been violated. Revelations of abuse are especially painful when they involve leaders who use God language to excuse their predation or shift blame to victims ("God said this was okay," "Ministry is lonely for me, so I need this," "We have a special spiritual bond," "You should forgive and move on"). Such actions are a scandal to the gospel, deserving of millstones (Matt. 18:6), and are grounds for permanent removal from ministry.

Not all abusers are celebrities. But celebrity power makes it much easier for someone to abuse, in a multitude of ways.

Celebrity leaders are often charismatic and charming. They can woo others with their words, persuade others to catch their vision, or simply light up a room with their smile and presence. It's easy to see how this interpersonal power can be used to manipulate. Celebrity amplifies the power differential upon which abuse feeds.

Celebrity attracts. People want to be around the celebrity because they are funny and smart or because their public output—via sermons, books, or comedy bits—has had a positive effect. In the cases of Crist, Hybels, Zacharias, and others besides, victims said they were initially excited to be close to the leader. There was something irresistible about being invited to hang out backstage, or on a yacht, or in the greenroom. It's flattering to join the celebrity's inner circle, however briefly. In addition, victims are sometimes lured by the promise that the celebrity can make *them* celebrities or help them with their careers.

Celebrity deceives. It whispers to the celebrity leader that they are above the rules, the morals, or the law. One of the most chilling distillations of this attitude comes from our former president: "When you're a star, they let you do it. You can do anything," he said, before bragging about assaulting women.[44] He said the horrible thing, but other presidents and countless other powerful men, judging by their actions, seem to believe this. They believe it because others have allowed them to operate outside normal bounds of integrity and accountability. If celebrity deceives the individual, it can also deceive a community or institution.

Celebrity shields. When victims come forward with allegations, the celebrity leader can rely on supporters and fans to take their side and discredit victims. The wealth that so often attends celebrity allows them to lawyer up for lawsuits or criminal charges. Or they can use their financial power to essentially buy victims' silence, in the form of out-of-court settlements, nondisclosure agreements, or both. Some victims decide that publicly standing up to their abuser just isn't worth it, given the backlash from fans and lengthy legal battles.

Finally, celebrity isolates. Many celebrity leaders find themselves disconnected from people who really know them. Without true proximity, celebrity leaders can get away with behavior that they'd never consider if others could find out. The space beyond the spotlight can be a dark place indeed. It can be lonely and disorienting. Needless to say, a travel schedule that takes someone from hotel to hotel, in towns with many adoring followers but no real friends, surrounded by an entourage, creates a breeding ground for deception and abuse.

In the case of Crist, one wonders whether during the eight months away from comedy, he took time to directly apologize to the women he hurt. One also wonders whether he's cut out to be a touring comedian, given that he previously used the isolation of life on the road to prey on people. For their part, many fans assured Crist he was forgiven, generically. They thanked him for returning to comedy so that they could laugh through the rough year that was 2020.[45]

It's tempting to conclude that a board or governing body would have kept Crist in check. That is, if only he had been embedded in an organization with a board or council to whom he answered, he might not have acted out. Without knowing Crist or his heart, and genuinely hoping for his repentance and healing for victims, I think building a career out of a one-man show is a unique recipe for disaster.

But we would be naïve to think that institutions always can or will prevent abuse. As chapter 2 discussed, the power of celebrity in our time has far eclipsed the power of institutions. Institutions often act as a platform for the celebrity's career or influence more than they are an arena of transparency and deep transformation. And when it comes to abuse, entire institutions can be duped into believing a false account. Institutions built around a celebrity figure and his legacy are uniquely susceptible to evading the truth of abuse, even when it's staring them in the face. At their worst, institutions can become an abuser's greatest enabler and accomplice.

When Institutions Abuse

The results of the investigation into allegations against Zacharias did not mince words. It found that he had preyed on several women working at the day spas he frequented. He exchanged explicit texts and images with women worldwide. He had told one woman, who accused him of rape, that she was his "reward" for living a life of faithful service and "made her pray with him to thank God for the 'opportunity' they both received."[46] And he had groomed Thompson to send him explicit photos as he "gained her trust as a spiritual guide, confidante, and notable Christian statesman."[47]

In response to the findings, RZIM's international board of directors released an open letter. Leaders expressed shock, grief, and sadness. Then they said something important, and unusual: "We also feel a deep need for corporate repentance."[48] The letter went on:

> We now know based on the investigation that Ravi engaged in a series of extensive measures to conceal his behavior from his family, colleagues, and friends. However, we also recognize that in situations of prolonged abuse, there often exist significant structural, policy, and cultural problems. . . .
>
> We regret that we allowed our misplaced trust in Ravi to result in him having less oversight and accountability than would have been wise and loving.[49]

It would have been easy for the board to claim ignorance. After all, only Zacharias had abused. He had ostensibly hidden his behavior from staff, supporters, and family. He had four mobile phones and refused to hand them over for examination.[50] He claimed to follow the Billy Graham Rule, but regularly met alone with female massage therapists for back problems. He often traveled 300 days a year, even while other staff were asked to limit their travel to 100 days a year. In sum, it's difficult to know just how much RZIM could have known about its founder. It seems Zacharias had perfected a life of secrecy.

Even still, the RZIM board rightly acknowledged that abuse isn't just an individual problem; often, it's an institutional problem. RZIM had refused to pursue the truth about its founder. Leaders had either turned a blind eye or trusted Zacharias's account without asking for more information. When allegations began to surface, most leaders believed Zacharias—that he was the victim of extortion, that Lori Anne and her husband were con artists, that no money had been exchanged with the Thompsons. (In fact, Zacharias had paid them $250,000 to settle out of court.) Leaders failed to launch an investigation when the Thompson story emerged in 2017. Later, when a few RZIM leaders pressed for more information, their reputations inside the organization were smeared.

For an apologetics ministry proclaiming to love truth, corporately, RZIM failed to pursue it. The reality is, many of us would do the same. It takes leaders of unusually strong character to hold a beloved figure to account, to entertain the possibility that they aren't who they say they are. Beyond the incredible cognitive dissonance this creates, we fear that if our leader or mentor is exposed, then our own attachment to them, and what they represent to us, will come apart. And what will that mean for our own calling or identity? Or we remember our own positive experiences with them and operate from a false moral binary: since we saw good, the person can only be *entirely* good, not *also* capable of hurting others or misusing their power.

In many organizations, toxic celebrity power doesn't start off as being about celebrity. It often starts as something akin to love—respect, perhaps, or admiration. We join an organization because we look up to the founder or top leader. We want to be like them or to carry on their important legacy. We derive a measure of our own identity and purpose from them.

That was initially true for Ruth Malhotra. She attended the same Georgia school that Zacharias's children attended, and she looked up to "Mr. Ravi."[51] As a young adult, she left a job in politics, feeling called to ministry. In 2013 she became RZIM's spokesperson, traveling with Zacharias to India on a speaking tour. But when she noticed him spending a day alone with a masseuse, she raised concerns. It didn't go over well. "I just learned to keep my mouth shut," she said.[52]

Four years later, when the Thompson story emerged, Malhotra joined an internal task force to navigate the crisis. When she noted some inconsistencies in Zacharias's story, she said she was "marginalized, maligned, and misrepresented to others by key members of senior leadership."[53] One leader called her "tired and emotional" and discouraged her from taking notes during the meetings. Another said she had moved from "being skeptical to being cynical." Another said that Malhotra needed to "do the Matthew 18 thing and go to Ravi directly." If she didn't, she would be "disobedient," because "that's what Jesus would do." Still another asked Malhotra repeatedly, "Whose side are you on?" when she asked hard questions. In addition to this pressure on Malhotra, staff would mock Thompson and boast of Zacharias's long marriage to his wife.[54]

On the other side of the Atlantic, Amy Orr-Ewing, then the Europe, Middle East, and Africa director for RZIM, was facing her own hurdles pursuing the truth. When she learned that Zacharias had signed a nondisclosure agreement with the Thompsons, including paying the financial settlement, even though she had been told that he hadn't, Orr-Ewing *did* do the Matthew 18 thing. She confronted Zacharias on a trip to Bangkok. "I presented it as being in his own self-interest to correct the record," she told me in a phone interview. "But after that meeting, I later discovered I was marked as someone who was disloyal, cynical—a gossip." Top leaders "were trying to put fear in anyone talking about any of this at all."

Eventually the RZIM internal task force brought in a Christian "conciliator." This was presented as a chance for group members to reconcile after some tense meetings. Instead, the conciliator acted to pressure Malhotra to stop asking questions. She said Malhotra was "one step away from complete and total insanity."[55] Malhotra was asked to spend a week of "intensive sessions" with the conciliator. Instead of reconciliation, the conciliator was hired to gaslight Malhotra on behalf of the organization.

Orr-Ewing, for her part, was also required to meet with the conciliator and several leaders, for seven hours a day over four days. She described it as a "psychological re-education," in which she was told she was a gossip and had caused disunity—and that if the conciliation "didn't work" it could get her fired. Orr-Ewing told me she needed trauma therapy to recover from PTSD-like symptoms. Later, a psychologist concluded that the so-called conciliation met the criteria of psychological torture.

Sexual abuse is damaging enough. Zacharias had abused many—probably more than we can know. But with its dogged protection of its founder, RZIM had arguably engaged in spiritual abuse: of Malhotra, Orr-Ewing, and other leaders who dared to ask for the truth. Spiritual abuse is "a form of emotional and psychological abuse. It is characterized by a systematic pattern of coercive and controlling behavior in a religious context."[56] The pressure to conform to group thinking, the use of sacred texts and teaching to stifle concerns being raised, and the belief that an abuser has a "divine" position can all be part of spiritual abuse. These were all evident in RZIM's treatment of these women.

Despite her hurts, Malhotra mourned that RZIM failed not only her but also, crucially, Zacharias. At some point, another leader could have sat down with Zacharias and asked for an account of the Thompson story that made sense. Or limited his use of cell phones. Or limited his travel, especially to undisclosed overseas locations. By acquiescing to his celebrity status, RZIM leaders had missed granting him a chance for genuine repentance. "Ravi was treated as an exception, he was placed on a pedestal, he was idolized," Malhotra wrote. "Tragically, that fed his narcissism and hindered the opportunity for repentance and rehabilitation."[57] She noted that he was not part of a local church and that he evaded accountability. Former RZIM apologist Daniel Gilman said he was "haunted by the fact that the apologists on our team are not simply apologists for Jesus but also for Ravi."[58]

"Ravi wasn't actually known by people," Orr-Ewing told me in our interview. "He was in a sort of category of his own."

When we put people in special, spiritual categories of power, without ensuring the proper accountability that all power requires—without insisting that they be known—we bear some of the blame when the powerful fall. When they fall, we fall with them. What's left is a shattered image and shattered lives. We've only begun to pick up the pieces.

5

Chasing Platforms

In the fifteen years I've worked as an editor in faith-based publishing, I've sometimes been asked, "So how do I get published?" Often it's at a writing conference, from a ministry leader or writer who feels they have an important message for the church. Sometimes I get private messages on social media that start "Hey girl!," after which an influencer hopeful asks me to help them meet an agent. (Reader, I do not help them.)

In all these cases, I believe *they* believe that God has given them a timely message and that a book or article could help people beyond their immediate scope of influence. Sometimes I'll explain how to create a book proposal or how to pitch an editor at a magazine. The publishing world can from the outside seem elitist or confusing, left to the subjective whims of editors or marketing teams. And because I've spent my career inside the publishing world, I'm often happy to advise those trying to faithfully navigate it.

But here's a secret: no matter how much they feel called to do so, or how strongly they believe God has given them an important message, I can't genuinely encourage most people to enter Christian book publishing.

It probably sounds odd, given that I am obviously happy to do the thing I'd tell many people not to do. It's especially odd given my current job as an acquisitions editor at a book publisher, where I am expressly responsible for persuading Christian leaders and thinkers to write books. It's like a chocolatier selling truffles that carry a warning label that processed sugar is bad. Or like a football coach recruiting new players, all the while telling them about the likelihood of traumatic brain injury. Aren't I participating in a culture and industry that perpetuates the problems I'm warning against?

Let me be clear from the outset: I serve in Christian book publishing because I believe in the value of Christian books. Every job in every industry requires wading into complex ethical waters, and the authors I get to work with are motivated by the right things: They want to help their readers. They have legitimately helpful information to share or a genuinely compelling story to tell. They, naturally, get paid for their work but are not in the industry to make a fortune.

That said, perhaps it's because I've seen Christian book publishing from the inside that I'd turn many author hopefuls away from it. The primary reason for my caution is that the book publishing industry—and the agents, publicists, brand consultants, social media managers, and conference organizers connected to it—has added jet fuel to the problem of Christian celebrity, to the tune of $1.22 billion in sales in 2018 alone.[1] Most Christian publishers are businesses, so they exist in large part to sell books and create profit. Religious publishing continues to grow despite the decline of national brick-and-mortar chains and the surge of online platforms and personalities.

Creating profit isn't bad. And many publishers are able to deftly balance questions of profitability with questions of writerly skill, training, and wisdom. But over time, like most institutions, publishers haven't been able to resist the ascendancy of celebrity in a consumerist culture. Today, platform, reach, and influence play an outsize role in determining who gets to write for the broader church. Institutions that an author belongs to become "platforms" from which to sell books rather than sacred communities where the rules of the market should be off limits. Author hopefuls, in response to publishers' demand for platform, will sometimes use marketing strategies and online tools to falsely amplify their influence to get publishers' attention. All the while, many readers are led to believe that authors are vetted for maturity, credibility, or theological acumen, when sometimes their book deal is the result of a social media team that knew how to crack an algorithm.

Plagiarism scandals among prominent Christian authors are only the most alarming examples of bad fruit born of an undue emphasis on profit and platform. Christine Caine, Mark Driscoll, and Tim Clinton have all faced allegations of "citation errors," or using someone else's words as their own. These stories don't just raise concerns about intellectual theft—a serious concern, to be sure. They also highlight the way modern celebrity can lure individuals and companies to skirt ethical standards while feeding the lucrative celebrity machine.

And like so many aspects of modern celebrity, it started out with good intentions.

People of the Book(s)

Evangelicals are book people. Of course, they are people of *the* Book, placing a high value on reading the Bible in private and communal settings. Gutenberg's printing press fueled the Protestant Reformation, allowing Scripture translations from Wycliffe, Tyndale, and Luther to make their way into people's homes and lives.[2] These Reformers encouraged a "plain reading of Scripture." They believed that God speaks to individuals by illuminating the Word through the Spirit, absent the mediating power of church authority.

When his German translation of the New Testament sold 5,000 copies in two weeks—decent sales even by today's standards—Martin Luther became the world's first bestselling author.[3] Ever since, many Christian authors have been trying to snag that "bestselling" title.

Evangelicals are also people who like books. In a mass-print culture, they "understand and approach the reading of books and Bibles as a primary practice of cultivating personal faith and individual intimacy with God."[4] When I became a Christian, it didn't take long to see the central role of books in my burgeoning faith. My youth pastor recommended *I Kissed Dating Goodbye*, the defining distillation of purity culture since Elisabeth Elliot's *Passion and Purity*. In 1999, I got up early at a friend's sleepover to pore over a *Time* cover story about the Columbine shooting. Shortly after, my mom gave me a copy of *She Said Yes: The Unlikely Martyrdom of Cassie Bernall*, who allegedly professed faith in God moments before her death. Before I headed to college, my mom also gave me Lauren Winner's *Girl Meets God: On the Path to a Spiritual Life* and Joshua Harris's *Boy Meets Girl*. (I'll let you guess which one I liked better.) In college, while mining the intellectual riches of the faith, I devoured the works of C. S. Lewis, Frederick Buechner, Karl Barth, Julian of Norwich, Fleming Rutledge, and Anne Lamott. For many Christians, reading is a spiritual act.

Reading is also a consumer act. Historian Daniel Vaca notes that today, "virtually all aspects of social life involve commodification and consumption," and that includes religious life.[5] We establish group identity and belonging, including spiritual identity and belonging, largely through the things we buy and the content we consume. Legacy Christian publishers such as Eerdmans, Zondervan, Moody, and Baker (the publisher of this book, as well as my employer) together have created a "commercial infrastructure" for modern Christian identity, more defining than any one denomination or organization.[6] In *Reading Evangelicals*, Daniel Silliman notes that publishers after World War II found sales potential in a "transdenominational" market. Since then, books about missionaries, dramatic conversions, and self-help on marriage and family have defined the Christian market, shaping evangelicals' identity and felt needs.[7]

Some top mainstream publishers—notably HarperCollins, owned by Rupert Murdoch's News Corp—have recognized the massive sales potential in faith-based publishing. Since Harper-Collins acquired Zondervan in 1988 and Thomas Nelson in 2011, half of Christian publishing is now owned by a multinational corporation that primarily exists to create a profit.[8]

In previous times, when institutional authority and identity held more cultural power, Christian publishers might have contracted books based on an author's training, experience, and ministry credentials. But nonfiction evangelical trade publishing today largely contracts books based on individual rather than institutional authority. This is not surprising, given the history reviewed in chapters 2 and 3 and the rise of individual authority over against institutions in all sectors of modern life. It's no surprise evangelical publishers choose to work with charismatic communicators who present a simple message of individual salvation via mass media. Evangelical readers—and thus the publishers who serve them—generally prefer individuals' stories of inspiration, advice, and life change over stories of institutions and church-based discipleship. Here is how Vaca puts it:

> Evangelical firms have valued celebrity status because it valorizes independent authority. Whereas older categories of status—such as "renown"—recognized people especially for serving well in esteemed social institutions and offices, the phenomenon of celebrity has directed admiration and imitation away from institutions and toward particular people for merit that they have seemed to deserve as individuals.[9]

"Renown" here could be a synonym for "fame." Fame comes as a by-product of virtue, wise leadership, specific accomplishments, or all of the above. It arises from acting and leading well in a particular embodied community, where someone knows others and can be known. By contrast, celebrity relies on mass media to create an aura of "well-knownness," as Daniel Boorstin puts it,[10] without the celebrity necessarily having to do anything noteworthy or virtuous. Celebrity is social power without proximity—the chance to influence without knowing or being known by those you are influencing.

Naturally, authors aren't going to know or be known by every one of their readers. It would be both weird and hypocritical for me to write a book that derides books as communication tools. The very nature of media is that it takes words and ideas beyond the confines of a time and place. That's indeed a gift; we wouldn't have many important, enriching works of insight and imagination without it. Further, we don't criticize Augustine for letting his writing take him away from the pastoral demands of Hippo.

But Augustine wasn't selling *Confessions* or his many other works to "fans." And he wasn't writing books as products to sell in the marketplace. It's our modern conflation of identity and gifting with a personal brand, and the endless quest for platform, that has compromised the original mission of Christian book publishing, and many authors besides. Discipleship is outsourced to gurus. Authentic relationship is mediated through "relatable" and vulnerable storytelling. And spiritual maturity is measured by the number of followers and books sold rather than by everyday integrity beyond the spotlight.

In summer 2019—more than twenty years after his bestseller thrust him into the national spotlight—Joshua Harris announced he was no longer a Christian. "I have undergone a massive shift in regard to my faith in Jesus," he wrote on Instagram. "The popular phrase for this is 'deconstruction,' the biblical phrase is 'falling away.'"[11] Two years later, after becoming a certified StoryBrand consultant with marketing guru Donald Miller, Harris launched a "deconstruction starter pack" online for $275. (The website said the fee would be waived for anyone who had been harmed by Harris's past teachings on purity.) The backlash was swift; Harris apologized and removed the course. Many critics felt Harris was trying to profit from people's pain; others, that he had barely done enough deconstructing to be an expert on it. While not a book, the starter pack highlighted how quick evangelicals—and former evangelicals—are to turn complex personal experience into a sellable product. "You can take the boy out of American celebrity evangelicalism, but you cannot take the American celebrity evangelicalism out of the boy," wrote Carl Trueman in a scathing essay. "Messianic self-confidence comes as standard. And the preacher is still both the salesman and the product being sold."[12]

"It's Always Been about Money"

I spoke with several leaders in Christian publishing to assess the role celebrity plays in our industry. They agreed to speak with me off record, because they wanted to keep their jobs and also because they felt some ambivalence about their role.

One acquisitions editor at a corporately owned publisher noted that celebrity has always shaped publishing. "Thirty years ago, it was Chuck Swindoll and James Dobson—whoever had the biggest radio show," she told me. "It's always been about money." Publishing is a business, and publishers naturally want to publish books that will sell. Audience size—whether radio listeners, TV viewers, or social media followers—is one way to assess sales potential. But today, she said, the pressure to sell is greater than ever, as more Christian publishers are owned by corporate giants. "Most people who work in editorial are believing Christians who want to publish good books," she told me. "But above them, if they're not in a place with a mission that's spiritually minded, it's about revenue."

The pressure to turn a profit gives platform an outsize role in who gets book deals. Quality of writing, educational credentials, and hard-won wisdom are not enough to get a contract. Writers are told they *must* also have platforms. Some author hopefuls find that creating a platform is like a second job. By contrast, someone with a large social media following, who can't write or doesn't have much to say, will find plenty of publishers and agents who want to publish their book. Numbers rule.

Even authors who are good writers and leaders can succumb to the numbers game. I have reviewed many proposals from author hopefuls with plenty of training and experience. They are good writers and sharp thinkers. But the marketing section of the proposal is often longer than the writing sample—if there is a writing sample. Other well-known pastors or leaders, with a hefty number of followers and supporters, are listed as people who can endorse and promote the book upon publication. To be fair, authors are simply playing by the rules that publishers and agents have set. But treating one's church as a prime consumer base, and ministry relationships as business transactions, shows that holy and set-apart things have succumbed to the insatiable demands of the marketplace.

"We love to bitch about empire, but in Christian publishing, we're in it," another longtime editor told me. He says the celebrity dynamic has mushroomed in recent years, in part because global conglomerates own half of the Christian publishing pie. Even as an industry veteran, he recently learned of a deal with a Christian publisher, and "my jaw dropped. I don't know how you would spend that money ever." He's concerned about the size of advances going to some Christian authors.

"If a typical Christian or even non-Christian reader were aware of some of those deals, they would ask: 'How is that Christian?'" he told me. "Even the most secular person would see that those dollar amounts aren't Christlike."

Since we're on the awkward topic of money, let's talk about advances. An advance is the money a publisher pays an author up front to write a book. Book publishing is a gamble, and publishers hope not only to recover the advance through sales but ideally to make a profit. Theoretically, an advance is determined by many factors: quality of writing, timeliness of topic, a particular editor's passion for an author or topic, and yes, author platform. From these factors, a publisher will create a sales forecast—how many copies it thinks it can sell. That forecast helps determine the advance amount.

All workers should be compensated for their work. And writing is work. (Listen, at this point in the manuscript— *believe me*, it's work.) Writing a book is a unique skill; few can do it well. It often requires research, interviews, and lots of time away from other responsibilities. Advances ensure that authors are paid for their work, regardless of how their book sells. As the recipient of two book advances, I am grateful for advances!

The problem, of course, is when advance amounts are determined mostly or solely by author platform—which is often shorthand for celebrity status—with relatively little weight placed upon quality of writing, freshness of ideas, and credentials. It's a self-fulfilling system: publishers invest more attention and money into authors they've already paid large advances to. Celebrity begets celebrity. "The larger advances create a gap . . . in the minds of employees," said the editor. "It allows preferential treatment." He's concerned that celebrity creates a tiered system among authors.

There's a power differential introduced too. When authors know their high value—literally, in the size of their advance— they are more likely to treat the publisher like a workhorse than a partner. Another agent and former longtime editor told me that in the past, he acquired books from three former celebrity pastors. "They were all bears to deal with, and their books never earned out," he said. When I asked what he meant by "bears," he answered, "Just huge egos." When publishers overpay for celebrities, he said, they squeeze out the chance for smaller authors with great writing and ideas to have a shot. Publishers can't help being sucked into the celebrity's self-orbit.

Some top-tier authors aren't authors at all. That is, they don't write the books that bear their names. Publishers are happy to let top "authors" hire a real author to write their books for them.

Ghostwriting is a common practice in book publishing. Today, ghostwriting even crops up with endorsements and forewords. In these cases, publishers—usually an editor or marketing team member—will write an endorsement for a celebrity leader, then run it by that leader to get their sign-off, like, "You'd say something like this, right?" Other times a celebrity endorser has their team or assistant read the book and submit an endorsement on their behalf. The celebrity endorser doesn't read the book that they are attaching their name to (which seems like a foolish practice—who knows what content you could be attaching your credibility to?).

When it comes to writing *books*, writing is a skill, and not everyone with a valuable message or story has it. (As the late Christopher Hitchens quipped, "Everyone has a book inside them, which is exactly where I think it should, in most cases, remain."[13]) It is my conviction that ghostwriting can be a perfectly acceptable practice, under two conditions: the person who puts pen to paper is (1) compensated at a level commensurate with the value they bring to the project; and (2) overtly credited. The unruly nature of celebrity in publishing means that some top bestselling authors are deemed too busy to write their own books—if they can write. And it often means that their ghostwriters are compensated *unfairly based on what the celebrity makes*, and *uncredited*.

All ghostwriters are paid something—usually by the author in a work-for-hire agreement. If a big-name "author" gets a $500,000 advance from a publisher, then pays the actual author $50,000, we might think that's a decent sum of money and a fair wage. But doesn't the actual author bring more than 10 percent of the value to the project? After all, the words on the page wouldn't exist without the blood, sweat, and tears of the ghostwriter. And if the book sells, the actual author won't be rewarded in royalties; the celebrity will. Compensation gaps of this nature reveal that the name of the "author" is valued at a higher level than the work of the actual author.

Then again, ghostwriters enter these agreements knowing full well that the celebrity is more valuable than their work. If they're happy with the pay, then we should let individuals go about their business, right? On one level, yes. Many ghostwriters are happy to help convey the message of the person they are writing for. Between the ghostwriter and the celebrity, it's a fine transaction. But when it comes to questions of credit, ghostwriting doesn't just involve two individuals in a private agreement. It also involves a reading public, people buying the book. Ghostwriting is fine as long as the buying public knows about the arrangement. Otherwise, it can be deceptive.

If you found out that your pastor didn't write their sermons or that your professor didn't write their lectures or that your favorite musician didn't write their lyrics—that they were presenting someone else's intellectual work as their own—you'd feel deceived and lied to, because you were in fact deceived and lied to. Such deception is grounds for firing or a lawsuit in other arenas. Yet the practice is common in publishing, including Christian publishing.

"When a pastor or ministry leader publishes a book with only his name on it, he is making an unstated promise to the reader that the material is his, it's coming directly from his heart and mind, and he's personally presenting it in the form of this book," notes Phil Cooke.[14] There is no reason Christian publishers and authors shouldn't credit ghostwriters for celebrity books. A simple "with" or "and" on a cover literally puts it up front. In fact, Christians should be the first to acknowledge that any creative endeavor takes a team to pull off—that "all true creation requires collaboration."[15] When the name on the cover doesn't match the name of the writer, publishers only amplify the celebrity "author" while devaluing the work of the real author. They also, ultimately, participate in idolatry—the idol is the brand and multiperson project that's presented as "Pastor Karl." But Pastor Karl wouldn't exist without a community supporting him at every step. The real Karl should tell us when Katie wrote his words.[16]

Plagiarism Problems

It's no coincidence that many plagiarism scandals in Christian publishing involve the use of just such a community—a research firm or team of assistants. In 2013, when instances of plagiarism were found in two of Mark Driscoll's books, Mars Hill staff said that "a team of people, including a research assistant," were the people who had failed to cite sources.[17] In this way, Driscoll could dodge the blame, and "Mark Driscoll" the brand could keep writing books.

A similar dynamic cropped up when Tim Clinton—president of the American Association of Christian Counselors—was accused of plagiarism in 2018. In response, a spokesperson said Clinton has published "countless articles and dozens of books, totaling hundreds of thousands of pages," and that "some of those works have involved more of his direct involvement than others since he has often been assisted by graduate students or research associates."[18] The response aptly highlights the role of celebrity. For it manages to at once inflate Clinton's importance—look how busy and productive he is—while downplaying his responsibility for the content of the books bearing his name.

A former publicist at a corporate Christian publisher remembers the "icky moment" when she questioned her role in the industry. An author had hired an outside firm to land his book on the *New York Times* bestseller list. The publisher had strongly discouraged him from doing so, but he did it anyway. It didn't work; the book didn't make the list. After publication, he and his team were upset with the publisher that the book hadn't performed as hoped. But that wasn't where the problems started. "It was the same book I tried to flag plagiarism for," she told me. When she noted her concerns, that the content was too similar to another book's, she got the sense from the editorial team that they didn't care to look into it; it was simply too late to deal with it.

World reported on which Christian publishers use software that can detect plagiarism in their books. It found that the bigger publishers "did not as a matter of habit, while smaller publishers did."[19] Reporter Emily Belz noted that many industry insiders want better software. But software alone won't fix plagiarism—which comes from the Latin *plagiarius*, meaning "kidnapper."[20] Industry leaders also must invest the time to vet work, especially from top authors, even when it might mean delaying the release date. Hitting that date is less important than holding one's authors to a higher standard.

The same due diligence is required in assessing author platforms. Before the internet, it was hard (though not impossible) to fake a platform. The number of church members, radio listeners, or donors claimed by an author could be vetted, through denominational counts or news reports or IRS filings. Today, however—when online presence is nearly nonnegotiable for getting a book deal—it's very easy for author hopefuls to buy a fake platform.

"A celebrity is one who actively chases the public eye, wooing the media and cultivating a network of supporting agencies and fellow stars that manufactures mass recognition."[21] This definition of celebrity comes from historian Kate Bowler in her excellent book *The Preacher's Wife: The Precarious Power of Evangelical Women Celebrities*. Bowler argues that Christian women, absent avenues for formal authority in many institutions, have turned to the marketplace to exercise gifts of teaching and encouragement. When gender roles limit what women can be and do in the church, the market stands at the ready to turn them into powerful communicators as well as successful brands.[22] Women like Joyce Meyer, Lysa TerKeurst, Christine Caine, and Victoria Osteen have used their natural teaching skills and clear passion for the church beyond its walls, becoming darlings of the Christian publishing world and the complementary Christian conference circuit.

Bowler's definition of "celebrity" underscores that modern celebrity, including Christian celebrity, can be easily manufactured. If anyone—especially young women who aspire to a teaching ministry—wanted to follow in these leaders' footsteps, it's never been easier to manufacture the appearance of acclaim. The pathway starts online, where anyone can set up a profile, buy followers, and start churning out inspirational content.

One editor at a Chicago-area Christian publisher told me about a social media manager hired by pastors and ministry leaders to create and run their Facebook pages. The manager "boosts" the page to international audiences, often in Asia or East Africa, for a fraction of the cost of boosting to North American audiences. Doing so generates thousands of likes and follows for his clients. But there's little to no engagement—meaning, responses from real people. That's because the accounts are fake or inactive. "People will pay tens of thousands of dollars to have half a million or a million likes," the editor told me. "That will open the doors to book deals and even jobs." An author can present these numbers in their book proposal, knowing it's unlikely a publisher will vet whether those followers are real people who would buy a book. When the editor confronted the social media manager, saying the practice was deceptive, the manager framed his activity as "global ministry."

Bot followers—literally robots—are "an algorithm that pretends to be a real person on the internet," says journalist Nick Bilton.[23] Instagram estimates that 95 million of its users are bots.[24] In the documentary *Fake Famous*, Bilton selects three aspiring influencers as an experiment in fabricating fame. He buys them social media followers and likes, creates photo shoots that appear to be in exotic locales, and even rents a private jet studio—a room made to look like the interior of a private airplane, replete with leather seats and champagne flutes. Over time, the influencers start garnering real followers, and more fake ones, in the hopes of getting sponsors, all-inclusive trips, or book deals and other media opportunities.

In recent years, companies have begun using auditing tools to see if influencers are buying fake followers. Websites like Social Audit Pro, FollowerCheck, IG Audit, Hypr, HypeAuditor, and Famoid run an automated check for suspicious activity. But publishers—and book buyers—can do their own audits of individual accounts. Here are common signs that someone has purchased fake followers to deceptively amplify their influence:

- The user's engagement is less than 1 percent. An average followers-to-likes ratio is 1 to 5 percent, meaning that 1 to 5 percent of all followers will like a post. For example, if a user has 100,000 followers, a typical post would get 1,000 to 5,000 likes. But if someone with 100,000 followers typically gets only 100 likes and no comments, it's likely that a lot of those followers are fake.
- The user's engagement is generic—comments such as "Amen!" "Yes!" or a smile emoji. (You can buy fake likes and comments, too.)
- The user is followed by lots of accounts with no photos or posts, or accounts with lots of random numbers in the username.
- The user's follower count spikes randomly, then levels off. (The spike indicates the time of purchasing the fake followers.)

Given how easy it is to fake an online following, it can be tempting for author hopefuls who are competing for the attention of brands or publishers. But let's be clear: it is not ministry, unless one feels called to share the gospel with robots. It is seeking to profit from falsified data, and is thus a form of lying. It's the digital equivalent of evangelists fudging the numbers on their crusade attendance or pastors inflating membership rolls. Just as book publishers should take time to investigate these numbers, they should also run social media audits on author hopefuls who boast high social media numbers in their proposals.

Yet even when someone's followers are all real, presenting one's organization—whether church, denomination, or ministry—as a consumer base can degrade the call of ministry. A young, charismatic pastor thirsty for a national platform will emphasize to agents and publishers how big or fast-growing his church is. Publishers look at those numbers, see potential book buyers, and offer a contract based in part on church size and the size of other churches in the pastor's denomination or social orbit. In some cases, the church will budget to buy the book in bulk, thus boosting sales and royalties earned. The church might do a teaching series from the book so that members buy it in order to follow along. To be sure, there's nothing wrong with churchgoers liking their pastor's teaching and buying his book. Writing is a legitimate form of teaching ministry, allowing leaders to reach more people beyond their local congregation. There's also nothing wrong with a church deciding to support the pastor by buying bulk quantities. But the arrangement could lead a pastor to think of their church less as people to shepherd and more as consumers to cater to. And it leads churchgoers to think of their pastor as a purveyor of inspirational content rather than a shepherd of souls. As Trueman said, "The preacher is . . . both the salesman and the product being sold."[25]

Sometimes churchgoers aren't in on the deal. That was the case when Mark and Grace Driscoll signed a $400,000 contract with Thomas Nelson in 2011 to publish a book on marriage.[26] According to a former Mars Hill staff member who spoke with me on the condition of anonymity, the publishing executive who pursued Driscoll knew about the church's plan to hire ResultSource and didn't intervene. ResultSource is a now-defunct marketing company that promised to help authors get their books on the *New York Times* bestseller list. Its strategy was to help authors—or their ministries or churches—buy large quantities of the books, but to divvy up these sales into chunks that made it appear that individuals were buying the books, thus evading detection by the *Times*. Ministry leaders Les and Leslie Parrott, David Jeremiah, and Perry Noble all confirmed they have used ResultSource.[27] Between an initial fee and bulk purchases, Mars Hill paid about $242,000 to ResultSource—$217,000 for the books at adjusted market prices, and $25,000 for ResultSource's services.[28] The church also agreed to buy 11,000 copies of the book at adjusted market prices. In early 2012, as part of a "new year, new you" marketing boost, and tied to a sermon series on improving one's marriage, *Real Marriage* spent one week on the *NYT* bestseller list.

It's not really news that the bestseller lists are easily manipulated; plenty of agencies help "move books through retail channels."[29] Bulk sales have been used to land books on the list since Donald Trump's *Art of the Deal* in 1987.[30] Further, agencies like ResultSource are not illegal. They're simply a way to game the system. But when tithe money helps buy a pastor's bulk sales, and when publishers turn a blind eye to these arrangements, the house of God can look more like a house of "men, merchants, and money."[31] A place that should be set apart, holy, becomes defiled by the demands of commerce—often without congregants knowing that is what's happening. This is what led

Jesus to make a whip and overthrow the tables of the money changers. We'd think Driscoll would have been paying close attention to the biblical story where Jesus fashioned a whip.

The former Mars Hill staff member recalled to me the day boxes of books started arriving at the church's bookstore, beyond the copies of *Real Marriage* that the church had agreed to buy. The bookstore manager was freaking out. "He said, 'We have almost double the amount of books I ordered. I ordered 10,000 copies, and we have those copies in boxes. But thousands and thousands of other copies keep coming in. Maybe I ordered incorrectly, but the order confirmation I received says 10,000 copies and at Mark's author discount.'" The store manager called the publisher, thinking this must have been a shipping error. That's when the manager, and other staff, learned for the first time that church money had been used to hire Result-Source and buy the books. "This was the smoking gun," said the former staff member. He left the following year.

ResultSource may be the most infamous deception in Christian publishing in the past decade. But we—book lovers, buyers, and publishers—would be remiss to simply chalk that story up to the excesses of a toxic church environment and its celebrity pastor. Even if our pastor isn't faking social media numbers or passing off someone else's content as their own, we have tacitly accepted that such practices are part and parcel of an industry where metrics of eternal worth are often subsumed into metrics of the market.

Books can change lives like few media can—that's why I wanted to be an editor in the first place. And that's why I mourn what much of Christian book publishing has become: a place where celebrity platform has taken over the conversation. It didn't have to be this way. Yet even discerning, spiritually sensitive editors are no match for the broader industry's push for bigger profits, shinier personal brands, and the all-consuming logic of late-modern capitalism. To be sure, plenty of individual leaders, and authors, in Christian book publishing stay in the industry to serve the church and amplify important messages, regardless of celebrity appeal. They have the right motives. But the pressure to create larger profits year after year often requires trading good motives for pragmatic market considerations. In our celebrity-obsessed age, celebrity sells. At the least, Christian book buyers should be aware of why certain authors get the privilege of publishing a book. It's not always because they are called. Sometimes it's simply that they have cultivated the impressive appearance of calling.

6

Creating Persona

Jackie (not her real name) remembers her job interview at the megachurch well. She and her husband had felt called to attend the church, located in a wealthy city in the South, a couple years prior. With a charismatic inflection to her faith, Jackie had begun praying for the pastor, waking up in the middle of the night to intercede for his ministry. It seemed God was calling her to support the growing church for special purposes.

Given how drawn Jackie felt to the church, the job interview was jarring. During the interview, the pastor told Jackie that he could be a jerk but that no one else could say that except him. He told her that if he wanted his drinks prepared in a certain way (nonalcoholic, to be clear), they had better be prepared that way. "There was an instant spirit of fear," Jackie told me. As part of her hiring, she was required to sign a nondisclosure agreement—a legally enforceable contract that said she would never speak of her experiences inside the church. NDAs of this sort are not uncommon at large churches with reputations to protect.

That spirit of fear continued for the two years Jackie worked at the church, where staff were on call to attend to the pastor's needs. Other leaders there created a culture of deference, such as standing whenever he walked in the room; the rationale was that, if top staff didn't show respect, how would church members? "I was told to try to think of anything that could be distracting and disruptive and hurt his feelings and remove it completely," she said.

Toward the end of her time on staff, Jackie recalls a red carpet being rolled out for the pastor—literally. Staff put a red carpet in the building and invited attendees to come get their picture taken with the pastor. When Jackie left, it was "an abrupt chop." Leaving the staff, even on decent terms, meant being cast out of the pastor's circle of trust.

Despite these unsettling experiences, and after years of healing from the toxicity of the church environment, today Jackie feels compassion for the pastor. She's seen videos of him preaching at a young age—"It was pure," she told me. She believes the pastor started with good motives but got lured into the spotlight, in no small part due to others who put him there too early, without the maturity needed for the role. She believes he has abandonment issues, the fear that he will be found out to be not enough amid pressure to lead the church, and therefore will be unloved and rejected. She confessed that she derived too much of her identity from being in his circle. "My identity came in being in the entourage and what I did for God and for this celebrity pastor as opposed to who I was in Christ," she told me. "And that's on me."

Hearing Jackie's story, and the stories of other famous Christian leaders, I'll admit that compassion isn't the first place I go. It's hard to feel sorry for leaders whose actions place them on the far end of the narcissism spectrum. It's hard to feel bad for leaders who use the gospel to accrue power for themselves rather than pour it out for others. It's especially hard to pity celebrity leaders when their actions have hurt so many. As the previous two chapters have made clear, the central concerns of this book are the abuses of power that celebrity feeds and the pursuit of platforms that celebrity demands.

But if celebrity is social power without proximity, celebrity leaves many a famous person very alone—with few people who know them in deep, abiding ways, which is how all people want to be known. With few relationships that will stick even when the spotlight fades or the ministry fails. With few friends who will celebrate them not for what they do but for who they are, the unvarnished, unimpressive parts and all.

Celebrities are people. And God made all people to be loved and known—to find relationships that reflect God in Christ's love for us. But celebrity power crowds out love. To be sure, it can certainly look and feel like love. When a group stands when you walk in the room, of course you'll feel admired. When thousands of fans bombard your social media feeds with hearts and buy your newest book or album, you'll feel good that so many people appreciate your work. When a conference attendee tells you that your message changed their life, before asking you to sign their copy of your book, you'll feel like you're really, finally, making a kingdom difference.

Together, the dynamics of fandom feed the need to feel seen, known, and loved. At least for a while. Put in a room of people who are eager to hear our insights or creative work, many of us could run on the fumes of adoration for a time. But like all idols, celebrity exacts a price. The feelings of love that it offers, over time, crowd out the actual love that requires proximity—if not daily proximity in the form of marriage or friendship, then certainly the proximity that can only come through vulnerability with other people for the long haul. Celebrity prevents many people from getting the deeper thing that made them seek celebrity in the first place: love and acceptance.

In this chapter, we'll examine the costs of celebrity *for* the celebrity. But we'll also examine why and how everyday Christians have placed the burden of celebrity on others, looking to famous Christian leaders to fulfill their spiritual and psychological needs. "Uneasy lies the head that wears a crown" is the most famous line from Shakespeare's *Henry IV*. Today, it also implicates those of us who have made others into kings and queens.

The Paradox of Loneliness

The first time I felt heartsick over a celebrity's death was in 2014. The headline read, "Philip Seymour Hoffman, Actor of Depth, Dies at 46."[1] Little about Hoffman's final days was known, but it seemed bleak, stemming from his struggles with addiction, something he spoke openly about. Hoffman was a feature in many films of my young adulthood: *Boogie Nights*, *Magnolia*, *The Big Lebowski*, and *The Talented Mr. Ripley* among them. Frumpy and lacking washboard abs, Hoffman was not a traditional leading man, but he was acclaimed for the pathos he brought to every role.

There were hidden reasons he did this so well. After his death, a friend of his observed, "[Hoffman] carried an unearned burden of shame. He was private, but he played those characters so well because he knew something about guilt and shame and suffering." In 2005, Hoffman said, "No one knows me. No one understands me. That's the other thing that changes as you get older. It's like everybody understands you. But no one understands me."[2] He was survived by his longtime partner and their three children.

The second time I felt heartsick over a celebrity's death was in 2016. Prince Rogers Nelson was found dead at age fifty-seven at his Paisley Park compound, after overdosing on a potent painkiller. Prince was almost otherworldly as a genre-bending (and gender-bending) singer, songwriter, and instrumentalist. He was both a Grammy-winning genius and an enigma whose playful, provocative music reshaped pop music. He was loud and swaggering on stage, and painfully private off stage. "Prince was odd and inscrutable to the end; he remains our unbelievable thing," wrote Vinson Cunningham. "Prince was a genius, but he was also, somehow, a person, just like us, and now he is gone."[3]

In his final days, Prince's few close friends knew he was struggling with dependence on painkillers due to pain in his hands. He said he was depressed and bored. He died alone.[4]

It's always a curious event when a celebrity dies. "Event" is the operative word here, because that's how media treat the death and how we consume the news. Celebrity deaths perform consistently well in the news cycle, all the more so if the death is tragic or involves someone young. Fixation on celebrity deaths has real-world consequences: long before the internet, celebrity suicides were shown to have a copycat effect.[5] Media push the ethical limits when they include lurid details of a person's death or milk the story long after the initial news.

But journalists are also simply responding to consumer appetites; they tell us what we want to hear. We are fascinated by celebrities as much when they are dead as when they're alive. Their final days or hours are offered as fodder to be consumed. Indeed, that's the only way we can engage their deaths, because we don't *know* an actual person to mourn. We know only what they presented to us on screen or on stage—that is, a sliver of the sum of their lives. When I mourned Hoffman's and Prince's deaths, I was mourning the way their art enriched my life and imagination. Those are valuable things to mourn; I and so many others remain grateful for their immense gifts. But it's not the same as mourning the full contours of a person.

We know our fascination with celebrity borders on idolatry because of the human toll it takes. It's almost axiomatic to note the costs of life in the spotlight, especially if you are very famous and very young. Daniel Radcliffe, best known for his titular role in the *Harry Potter* films, recalls being booed and shouted at as a child traveling with his parents overseas. As a teenager, he turned to alcohol to cope with the decidedly unmagical parts of too-young stardom.[6] Britney Spears, Macaulay Culkin, Lindsay Lohan, Amy Winehouse, Corey Haim, and River Phoenix have all paid the price of young fame. Stefani Germanotta (Lady Gaga) has spoken of feeling trapped in her home, since going out usually brings out the hordes and paparazzi. "I don't think I could think of a single thing that's more isolating than being famous," she said. What's isolating is that most people interact with her as a goddess rather than a human being.[7] Several years ago, Justin Bieber created a "no pictures" policy with fans, because "it has gotten to the point that people won't even say hi to me or recognize me as a human. I feel like a zoo animal."[8]

One common theme of superstardom is the paradox of loneliness: that the more that people know *of* you, the less that people can know *you*. Many celebrities say they keep their inner circle very small for fear of being stalked, harassed, or used by hangers-on. It's hard to have an intimate conversation with a bodyguard standing nearby. Others find that dating and meeting new people is awkward (and not in the charming, foppish way of *Notting Hill*). Romance is fodder for tabloids and exploitative bloggers, every new relationship and breakup a clickable headline. There's even a perverse desire to see celebrities suffer, because it convinces us that they're "just like us"—and that our private suffering is not so bad as their public kind.

In a 2009 study of American celebrities, psychologist Donna Rockwell found that celebrity status results in a kind of death—an "irreversible existential alteration" that includes loss of privacy and freedom to go about life with anonymity. The famous, she found, are alone on the "island of recognition," where they find "a loneliness that happens because you are separate."[9] Adoration entails separation—you are above mere mortals and therefore untouchable, set apart from everyone else. Because of this, it's not actually very nice to adore someone without the attendant knowledge of their foibles and a commitment to love them for the long haul.

Many famous people cope by using what Rockwell calls "character-splitting." They craft a "celebrity entity," a presentation of the self, while the true self is hidden away, shown only to trusted friends and family. Character splitting is in some ways healthy; the famous person realizes there is a vulnerable, beloved self that should be protected from overexposure. We are all more than the sum of our achievements and the acclaim that accompanies them. We all need communities that promise to love us instead of adore us.

At the same time, character splitting leaves room for a divided self, which is to say, a lack of integrity. Integrity means *integration*, but many celebrities, whether in Hollywood or the church, feel divided from within. The "celebrity entity" knows how to act to keep the watching public satisfied, but the true self might be crumbling, longing for a normal life. The true self might not even like the celebrity entity all that much. Yet the adoration bestowed on the celebrity entity can be intoxicating; one person told Rockwell, "I've been addicted to almost every substance known to man at one point or another, and the most addicting of them all is *fame*."[10]

Another word for this public-facing "celebrity entity" is "persona." *Persona* comes from the Latin, meaning "mask" or "character played by an actor," but it's certainly not relegated to the stage. A persona is the self-presentation that all of us take on in various settings and roles. It's closely related to the notion of personality—the set of qualities, traits, and quirks that together make you "you." Some personality traits are ingrained, while many are learned early on, based on the roles we were expected or needed to play in our family or community. Our personality is how we learned, early on, to get our needs met for love, security, and belonging.

Twentieth-century philosopher Hannah Arendt said that a persona is the mask through which our true selves "sound through." In a 1975 speech, she said:

> "Persona" . . . originally referred to the actor's mask that covered his individual "personal" face and indicated to the spectator the role and the part of the actor in the play. But in this mask, which was designed and determined by the play, there existed a broad opening at the place of the mouth through which the individual, undisguised voice of the actor could sound.[11]

Arendt believed that our persona is necessary for fulfilling our responsibilities in the world. But it's not ultimate. Despite the global recognition she received for her writing, she looked forward to obscurity, to a day when she could exist in her "naked 'thisness' . . . not seduced by the great temptation of recognition which, in no matter what form, can only recognize us as such and such, that is, something which we fundamentally are not."[12] This "naked thisness" is another way of saying our true self—the self who is created, held, and sustained by the living God, compared with the false self of ego, hustle, and image management.

The Loneliest People in the World

There are costs when Christians fall for "the great temptation of recognition" and grow disconnected from their belovedness in Christ. Chuck DeGroat has seen the costs up close. A clinical psychologist, seminary professor, and expert on narcissism in the church, DeGroat counsels many leaders in high-pressure roles. They come to him after burnout or moral failure or when their work is taking a toll on their health or family. They find it exhausting to maintain their persona among their peers or organization. The persona is killing the person underneath.

"Underneath that part that needs to show up well, [they are] compensating for loneliness, shame, insecurity," DeGroat told me in a phone interview. "The pressure is, 'I have to day in and day out deliver, I have to perform, I might lose them, but I might also lose myself, because I've only known myself as one who performs.'"[13] Some leaders don't know their worth apart from the role they play; if the persona is stripped away, it feels like their value in the world will go with it. The leader out of touch with their true self will cling to the spotlight, even to their own and others' detriment, because it's the only way they know how to feel love.

Since he wrote a great book on the topic, DeGroat and I discussed narcissism among Christian leaders.[14] For many fallen Christian celebrities, those who worked closely with the leader thought the problems traced back to his or her narcissism. The term is bandied about a lot, but it's important to distinguish between narcissistic personality disorder (NPD) and simply what DeGroat calls a leadership "style." NPD is difficult to diagnose and treat; an estimated 0.5 percent to 5 percent of the US population has it.[15] There's no great research today on how common NPD is among Christian leaders.

DeGroat defines NPD from a clinical perspective as "a grandiose sense of one's self, a lack of empathy for others, an entitlement to affirmation or attention, and ruptures in family and work relationships."[16] Other characteristics include avoiding responsibility, taking credit for others' work, seeking revenge, using verbal threats to control others, and exaggerating accomplishments. These behaviors are meant to "hide the self from others."[17] People with NPD find authentic relationships very difficult.

Important, for our purposes, is that the narcissist doesn't know who they are apart from what others reflect back to them. That reflection is the only way they know their worth. Like Narcissus stuck at the water's edge, they are terrified to step away from the pool—be it the stage or their publishing platform—that reflects praise. They are incapable of empathy because they can't imagine others' pain, and that's because they don't have access to their own. Clinicians say there's no "healing" NPD, although change is possible. "Narcissists are the loneliest people on the planet," DeGroat told me.

Of course, someone can have narcissistic tendencies without being diagnosed with NPD. DeGroat has used the Millon

Clinical Multiaxial Inventory—an assessment tool of personality disorders—with hundreds of pastors. He said many (though not all) show what he called an "elevation" around the characteristics of grandiosity and entitlement. The pastors who become healthy—who can move beyond a persona, get in touch with their true self, and lead from integrity and humility—are the ones who expect they might have these tendencies and want to address them. The fact that they are meeting with DeGroat is a hopeful sign.

Another hopeful sign is a willingness to examine past trauma. Sometimes pastors are bullies, for example, because they were bullied earlier in life. Moving past persona means getting in touch with their pain and the less shiny parts of their story. Another hopeful sign is a choice to surround themselves with people who can answer the question, "How do you experience me?" Healthy leaders seek out confidants who aren't hired to puff up their ego, who will honestly tell them if they are acting grandiose or entitled. Put another way, they need people who will see beyond the persona, who will name the messier parts of the true self—not to call out or condemn but to love and transform.

In light of recent, highly publicized ministry scandals, much has been said about accountability. Most churches say it's a top value, and they point to an elder board or denominational body to show they practice it. Outside church structures, many evangelical male leaders meet regularly to confess sexual temptation to each other. All of this is good, but it's not enough. We've seen that leaders can perform submission without really submitting. A board can be stacked with buddies. An accountability meeting between pastors can devolve into blowing off steam about irksome members. And we saw in chapters 3 and 4 that the power differential between a celebrity leader and board members can make it hard for the latter to speak honestly. Think about meeting with your boss—an impressive, intelligent leader you admire who also happens to be stressed and sometimes short-tempered—and directly naming their sins and shortcomings. If you're not squirming a bit imagining it, you are either very brave or have a great boss.

Further, according to DeGroat, narcissistic leaders tend to be "ecclesiastical loners." According to sociologist Robert Enroth, they evade checks and balances and prefer to operate independently, as a "one-man (or one-woman) spiritual show."[18] Their church or organization is an extension of their ego, and members gravitate to it to meet their own need for validation. There is such a thing as collective narcissism, wherein a "mutually enforcing relationship exists between leader and follower."[19] Drawing on the work of psychiatrist Jerrold M. Post—who diagnosed collective narcissism as a function of modern politics—DeGroat writes:

> The leader relies on the adoration and respect of his followers; the follower is attracted to the omnipotence and charisma of the leader. The leader uses polarizing rhetoric that identifies an outside enemy, bringing together leader and followers on a grandiose mission. The followers feed off the leader's certainty in order to fill their own empty senses of self. Interestingly, in this mutually enforcing relationship, both are prone to a form of narcissism.[20]

I imagine many of you readers have been part of a spiritual community where collective narcissism was at work. If so, you know how hard it is to inject accountability into a spiritual body centered on a leader with narcissistic tendencies, to change church cultures that are built around their persona. As long as we followers derive a sense of spiritual mission from our attachment to this leader, we'll be reluctant to dethrone them. If they step down, we wonder if the church—and our own sense of living on fire for God—will survive.

One measure of true accountability for church leaders is how they feel about it. Basically, it should hurt a little. I'm reminded of C. S. Lewis's advice on giving: "If our charities do not at all pinch or hamper us, I should say they are too small. There ought to be things we should like to do and cannot do because our charitable expenditure excludes them."[21] Likewise, there should be things the Christian leader would like to do but can't because colleagues and friends advise against it, or because they know themselves well enough to know that more power and fame will isolate them from their true, beloved self and could hurt others in the process. A little pinching of the ego is good for us all.

Rich Villodas, pastor of a large, diverse church in New York City, insists that congregations make sure their leaders are *accessible* and *accountable*—meaning they have social power *with* proximity. Here's what Villodas writes about accountability:

> I would be lying if I told you I do this joyfully. I don't like being told what to do. I want to call the shots. I want to inform people, not ask for permission. Yet this has been one of the most important safeguards for my leadership and pastoral life.
>
> I'm grateful to report to an elder board that asks hard questions monthly. I'm grateful that they are not "impressed" with me. In the past couple of years, I've had to grow significantly in my relationship with the board. To this day, submitting to

healthy authority is a struggle for me. My false self is exposed. My perfectionism is clearly seen. Yet deep down inside, I know God is protecting me.[22]

The path away from persona and toward the true self is the path of humility. And humility usually requires some form of *humiliation*—stripping away the stories we tell ourselves to reveal a more vulnerable creature. It's not a popular path; most pastors choose to stay in the pulpit, despite criticisms, pressure to always have the right answers, and isolation that comes from keeping up the false self. In 2015, LifeWay Research found that only about 13 percent of pastors had left the pastorate in the last decade for reasons other than death and retirement.[23] Of course, this was before 2020, when many churches juggled ideological conflict, virtual worship amid a global pandemic, and a polarizing news cycle. There's some initial evidence that more pastors in 2020 and 2021 were flaming out of ministry.[24] In spring 2020, Barna found that about one in five pastors "frequently" felt lonely within the past month, while LifeWay found in 2011 that of 1,000 pastors surveyed, 55 percent said they felt lonely at times, with loneliness increasing among pastors of large churches.[25]

Burnout often occurs amid the demands of a high-pressure role without a place to be vulnerable. Sometimes leaving the spotlight, stepping into a smaller one, or having it taken away— whether by choice or by fiat—is the best thing that can happen. Henri Nouwen was one of the few to take this path less traveled. In the book *In the Name of Jesus: Reflections on Christian Leadership*, he recounts how he had spent twenty years as a renowned scholar of pastoral psychology and spirituality, revered among fellow Catholics and Protestants alike. He was celebrated and successful. But after teaching at Yale, then Harvard, he experienced "a deep inner threat":

> After twenty five years of priesthood, I found myself praying poorly, living somewhat isolated from other people, and very preoccupied with burning issues. Everyone was saying that I was doing really well, but something inside me was telling me that my success was putting my own soul in danger.[26]

Note the painful mix of praise and isolation: Many people told Nouwen that he was doing great, yet he felt disconnected from others. The *persona* was thriving, but the person underneath was nearing what he would later call a spiritual death. Then he felt that God intervened—not with a weekend retreat or sabbatical, but by inviting Nouwen to leave public ministry altogether. Nouwen spent the next several years at L'Arche, an intentional community in France. There, people with intellectual disabilities and those without intellectual disabilities live and work together. Nouwen was asked to care for a young man named Adam. Having no ability to walk or speak, Adam modeled back to him a relationship of vulnerability and care. Adam was an icon for Nouwen of belovedness—a delighting in the self that is rooted in God's love alone. Nouwen wasn't a famous Catholic scholar among his new neighbors. He was, simply and blessedly, Henri. It reset his entire spiritual frame and sense of vocation. Obscurity reconnected him with his true, beloved self. It saved him.

Obscurity would be easier for many celebrities if we didn't need something from them. As it turns out, the costs of celebrity implicate us, the fans and consumers. We feed celebrity by turning to famous people to meet our own social and emotional needs.

When Fans Get Weird

If you spent any time online in 2021, chances are you saw headlines about stand-up comedian John Mulaney. And if you saw that news, you likely saw the term "parasocial relationships" thrown about.

Then again, maybe you didn't follow the news as closely as I did. I'll admit, reader: I am a *fan* of John Mulaney's. He is impossibly tall and smart, a Chicago native who grew up Catholic with two lawyer parents. (With a setup like that, how could you *not* become a comedian?) He has impeccable comedic rhythm; no second is wasted, and his tall and lanky body only adds to the effect. His material thrives on nice guy, wife guy energy, which is rare among stand-up comedians. He doesn't take cheap shots. I have watched his Netflix specials exactly thirty-seven times, which explains why many of his bits live in my head rent-free. (The real estate agent with fun mom energy, the horse loose in the hospital, and Mick Jagger's "not funny!" are recurring favorites.)

I'm not someone who fixates on celebrities' personal lives. Mostly, I can enjoy what certain actors or musicians do with their talents and leave it at that. This has turned out not to be the case with Mulaney, for me and a lot of other people. Following the news that he had spent time in a rehab program in late 2020, fans learned that he and his wife were divorcing. Then headlines announced that Mulaney was dating actress Olivia Munn. Naturally, many speculated about the connection between these headlines. Then we learned that Mulaney and Munn were having a child together. In the grand scheme of things, these are big and yet not entirely wild things to happen in someone's life. Yet a lot of people had big feelings about Mulaney's life direction. Writer Kayleigh Donaldson notes:

Even in the context of the typical brand of performative hyperbole that makes up the dominant language of social media, the responses to Mulaney's split and new love seemed unusually frantic. Some cried that love was dead. Others lamented how Mulaney didn't seem like that kind of guy. He just loved his wife so much. How could he do this to her? How could he do this to us?[27]

In other words, many fans felt personally hurt by decisions that didn't actually impact their lives at all. They felt disappointed, angry, and betrayed by Mulaney's life decisions—even while some recognized that these emotions were inappropriate. There was a pervasive sense that we *knew* Mulaney and thus had certain expectations for him, in part because he talked about his marriage and addictions in his routines. We seemed to have forgotten that comedy, like all art forms, requires a curated presentation of the self: a persona that masks a complicated person underneath. That many of Mulaney's fans forget it's all an act shows that he's just that good at it.

In a time when celebrities use social media to share intimate details of their lives, it's easy for fans to think they know their favorite actors and musicians, and even to come to expect celebrities to self-disclose. But the blurring between the personal and public lives of famous people started long before Instagram. The term "parasocial relationship" was coined by psychologists Donald Horton and R. Richard Wohl in 1956 to describe how media gives "the illusion of face-to-face relationship with the performer."[28] Television, radio, and film provide an unusually intimate encounter with celebrity personas:

The persona is the typical and indigenous figure of the social scene presented by radio and television. To say that he is familiar and intimate is to use pale and feeble language for the pervasiveness and closeness with which multitudes feel his presence.[29]

In other words, these media give viewers feelings of intimacy. In response, viewers emotionally attach to the persona in ways that are intense, even if not grounded in real relationship:

> The spectacular fact about such personae is that they can claim and achieve an intimacy with what are literally crowds of strangers, and this intimacy, even if it is an imitation and a shadow of what is ordinarily meant by that word, is extremely influential with, and satisfying for, the great numbers who willingly receive it and share in it. They "know" such a persona in somewhat the same way they know their chosen friends: through direct observation and interpretation of his appearance, his gestures and voice, his conversation and conduct in a variety of situations.[30]

A celebrity can create feelings of intimacy with crowds of strangers. In this way, celebrities hold immense power over our hearts and imaginations. But a parasocial relationship is inherently one-sided. The celebrity doesn't know you at all. They probably don't want to. The connection exists only in fans' minds. Even still, the *feelings* the parasocial attachment produces are real.[31] They can even be more powerful than real-life attachments, especially if someone's real life is affected by family breakdown, trauma, or isolation.

Psychologists say parasocial relationships can be healthy, as long as fans acknowledge that these relationships aren't rooted in true knowledge of the celebrity. They can allow people to figure out what values are important to them or help them develop their identity in ways that mimic a celebrity's. In the case of Mulaney, fans felt betrayed by his divorce and ensuing relationship because they valued his nice-guy persona. They (especially, perhaps, straight female fans) attached to him because they are looking for a man who likes being a husband. Fans struggling with addiction admired Mulaney for the way he had battled substance abuse in years prior. The onstage Mulaney was a romantic ideal and a role model. He reminded many of us of what we wanted to be or who we wanted to be *with*. When the onstage Mulaney went off script, divorcing and relapsing, the ideal crumbled.

As we discussed in chapter 1, celebrity worship belies a spiritual hunger in a time when traditional forms of worship and community are declining. Celebrities can "arouse the religious passions of followers in modern society who find spiritual meaning, personal fulfillment, and awe-inspiring motivation in the presence of these idols."[32] In the same way, parasocial relationships reveal a relational hunger in a time of individualism and loneliness. They give fans feelings of attachment when real attachments seem scarce. My friends might move to another city, get married, or hurt me, but at least I'll always have my other *Friends*. Another dinner alone goes down easier with another Kardashian drama playing in the background. I can lose myself in dramatic headlines about my favorite actor or musician to distract myself from the tedium and loneliness of my own life. Maybe I followed the Mulaney drama because my day-to-day life is decidedly undramatic. When real relationships fail us—as they inevitably do—parasocial relationships fill the void.

Christians should be the first to insist on the primacy of in-person relationship. We worship a God who took in-person relationship seriously—so seriously that he was born incarnate to an unwed mother in the backwaters of an ancient Roman province to get close to us. In response to Jesus's life, death, and resurrection, early believers formed intimate communities of solidarity and self-sacrifice, where leaders lived in proximity with their followers. They met together daily, pooled their resources to provide for those in need, and ate together in their homes, "with glad and sincere hearts" (Acts 2:46). At its best, the local church is the place where loneliness and isolation are replaced with real, vulnerable relationships—for leaders as well as for members.

So why do Christians keep putting people on pedestals, asking them to fulfill their own parasocial needs? Why do we turn our leaders into untouchable personas rather than letting them live and serve as their true, beloved selves? Why do our icons so easily become idols?

The answer, it turns out, takes us back to DC Talk, Joshua Harris, and other Christian celebrities of my adolescent faith. When Christians feed on a story of persecution and cultural embattlement, they're prone to take any Christian in the public spotlight as a kingdom win.

PART 3

THE WAY UP IS DOWN

7

Seeking Brand Ambassadors

In 2019, Kanye West made an unexpected career change: he got cozy with evangelical Christians. The popular hip-hop artist had just released his ninth studio album. Its title sounded like a billboard spotted along the long, flat highways of the Midwest: *Jesus Is King.*

Wow. God got one of the big ones.

It wasn't actually the first time West had rapped about Jesus. In the 2004 hit "Jesus Walks," West imagines what it would be like if Christ showed up in the club. I listened to that song, and the album it was on, a lot as a young adult. I enjoyed West's clever sampling and lyrics. I was also pleased that a talented artist would speak well of Christian faith—*my* Christian faith. West wasn't in the CCM bubble, after all. He had mainstream credibility, hailed by *Vibe, Rolling Stone,* and Pitchfork as the future of hip-hop. (He agreed, saying that "anyone who doesn't give [*The College Dropout*] a perfect score is lowering the integrity of the magazine."[1]) He had credibility in the broader world and might lend Jesus some credibility too.

One slight problem: West didn't rap *just* about Jesus. His debut album was also about drugs, sex, and luxury clothing and cars. Those were consistent themes on the rest of West's acclaimed, if uneven, albums. Self-worship was a theme—a pretty literal one. On *Yeezus*, he rapped, "I am a god." It's a bold thing to say, and also more or less what we'd expect from an egomaniac. Yet in a real way, West was telling the truth. Carrie Battan wrote in the *New Yorker*, "As a tormented genius who'd defied expectations and successfully transformed himself . . . to a rap icon and footwear-industry titan, West was as close to a secular god as there was, with millions of worshipful followers behind him."[2]

Then, in 2019, West found a God worthier of worship than himself. That year, he said, he finally gave his life to Christ. His then wife, Kim Kardashian, confirmed his conversion: "He has had an amazing evolution of being born again and being saved by Christ."[3]

"I tried it my way, it's not working out," he said. "Everything is in shambles. I'm ending up in debt, making this money but still ending up in debt. . . . I'm having ups and downs with my health. People calling me crazy. People not wanting to sit with me. I had to just give it up to God."[4] He said Christ had healed his addictions to alcohol and pornography. After his conversion, West started hosting "Sunday Services" at his estate, broadcasting them on social media. The highly produced concert experiences featured a gospel choir, messages from celebrity pastors Rich Wilkerson Jr. and Carl Lentz, and plenty of other celebrities besides. Even Brad Pitt showed up one weekend.

West's aims were explicitly evangelistic. At one Sunday Service, he even rewrote the lyrics of secular songs, à la all overeager youth pastors of the '90s. He performed a version of Nirvana's "Smells like Teen Spirit" with the lyrics, "Let your light shine, it's contagious / here we are now, inspiration."[5]

Jesus Is King released shortly after West started hosting his Sunday Services. It features a blend of soul, hip-hop, and house music, with lyrics that proclaim West's new mission to share the gospel. Once he gave Chick-fil-A a shout-out in one of his lyrics, he would always have an in with a large segment of white evangelicals.

The album debuted at number one on the Billboard 200 charts and won Best Contemporary Christian Music Album at the Grammys. Mainstream critics gave it generally warm reviews. Many Christians liked it too. The sex, drugs, and self-worship had been scrubbed away; finally, many white Christians could listen to rap without troubled consciences. In place of the typical profanity seemed to be a genuine testimony of a life changed by God. *Christianity Today*, The Gospel Coalition, even the typically dour *Plugged In* praised the album.

Christian leaders also encouraged us to see West's conversion as sincere. After all, the Bible and church history are rife with dramatic conversions. God continues to work in surprising ways, among people who seem the farthest from him. Besides, who else might be saved after listening to *Jesus Is King*? Would Brad Pitt be next? (Let me know if you want to visit my church, Mr. Pitt.)

Of course, none of us can know the content of West's faith. The only "Kanye West" we can know is the one presented on stage and on screens. West has a louder-than-life persona; he enjoys stirring controversy and defying expectations. It's possible that his Christian phase will be just that—a phase to try on before adopting another one. Nonetheless, it makes sense for

Christians to celebrate anyone coming to Christ, even if they can't "know someone's heart." Christians believe that wealth, success, and adoring fans are no match for the good news of salvation. Conversion stories—especially dramatic ones—are the heartbeat of evangelical faith.

But there are other reasons evangelical Christians might be eager to see celebrities proclaim Christ. With celebrity conversions, many Christians feel that their faith is being validated in realms that otherwise appear hostile or indifferent to their deepest beliefs. If Christians perceive that they are embattled in a secular culture, then celebrity conversions suggest that God's side might be winning—and that Christians in Hollywood or the music industry could have a positive influence in "dark" places. Christians finally have their ambassadors in the echelons of power, in places where Christians feel left out.

Besides, celebrity conversions make Christianity cool again.

A Holy War

Before Kanye West, there was Bob Dylan. It's hard to imagine a more different musical comparison. Yet they share one significant thread: they both professed a sincere Christian conversion and had the music to show for it.

The most important songwriter of the twentieth century, Dylan (born Robert Zimmerman) was raised in a Jewish family in Minnesota. After moving to New York as a young man, he became a staple of the 1960s antiwar movement, drawing on biblical imagery to express prophetic protest. Acclaimed albums like *Highway 61 Revisited*, *Blonde on Blonde*, and *Blood on the Tracks* captured the heady and turbulent political shifts of the late '60s and '70s.

Then, in 1978, Dylan allegedly began attending a Bible course at Calvary Chapel, a charismatic church in California, and got baptized in the Pacific Ocean. He told the *Los Angeles Times*, "I truly had a born-again experience, if you want to call it that. It's an overused term, but it's something that people can relate to."[6] His next three albums—*Slow Train Coming* (1979), *Saved* (1980), and *Shot of Love* (1981)—became known as his born-again trilogy. *Slow Train Coming* opens with the evangelistic "Gotta Serve Somebody." Christian rocker Larry Norman recommended it to President Jimmy Carter.

Around this time, Dylan began giving "nightly sermons" on tour.[7] Instead of speaking of the Vietnam War, he was now speaking of a cosmic war between good and evil, capturing the end-times theology of the time. "I'm telling you now, Jesus is coming back, and he is!" he declared. "There is no other way of salvation."[8] Not all his fans liked it, of course. Some felt betrayed. "Dylan represented free-thinking, anti-establishment values, you know, 'don't follow leaders.' And here he was following the ultimate leader," said journalist Michael Simmons.[9] Apparently at one concert, a sign could be seen in the agitated crowd: "Jesus loves your old songs."[10]

Even still, the backlash was evidence of sincere faith. After all, Jesus warned his followers that the world would mock and persecute them. In the song "Property of Jesus," Dylan tells of a man who is resented and called a loser because of his faith. Persecution, Armageddon, and spiritual warfare are regular themes on his Christian albums. This is no coincidence. With *The Late Great Planet Earth* and *A Thief in the Night*, the broader evangelical world of the time was obsessed with all things end times. National and global events were read back into the Bible, with certain political leaders as obvious stand-ins for the antichrist.

Dylan came to faith during the nascency of the religious right. The laid-back Jesus People of the '60s and early '70s had morphed into politically engaged warriors for truth and family values. Anita Bryant launched her anti-gay-rights campaign in 1977. Jerry Falwell cofounded the Moral Majority two years later. The pro-life movement was gaining traction as GOP leaders realized they could use the issue of abortion to attract and energize white evangelical voters. Indeed, many Christians were concerned about the fallout of the sexual revolution: higher divorce rates, the legalization of abortion, women working outside the home, and LGBTQ rights. To them, such cultural changes signaled the country's moral decline and, possibly, that the end was nigh. As Falwell told his Lynchburg church in 1980, "We're fighting a holy war. . . . We have to lead the nation back to the moral stance that made America great. . . . We need to wield influence on those who govern us."[11]

Christians were not to retreat from this holy war. They were to stand against the tides of broader cultural decay, to win the country back for God. At the same time, it was understood that to fight this war, they needed to adopt the tactics of their enemies, by gaining political and cultural influence. This holy war would ultimately be fought at the ballot box and through key alliances with public figures, not primarily through discipleship or the regular witness of the local church.

Dylan, for his part, critiqued the Moral Majority in 1980. "I think people have to be careful about all that. . . . It's real dangerous."[12] But even without him meaning to, his newfound faith reflected the concerns of Christians alienated by cultural shifts. Aaron Sanchez writes,

Dylan's Christianity had less in common with [civil rights leader] Jesse Jackson's and more in common with Jerry Falwell's. It fit comfortably within the perspectives of a reactionary Christianity that blamed liberalism and the Civil Rights movement for the nation's religious, moral, and economic decline. The end times were near and the nation needed to prepare for God's wrath.[13]

Dylan's faith remains a topic of interest. Some suspect that he returned to his Jewish roots in 1983, when his lyrics became vaguely spiritual and less Jesus-y. Others, like biographer Scott M. Marshall, believe that Dylan never abandoned Christianity entirely.[14]

To this day, at least three different pastors take credit for leading Dylan to Christ.[15] It's a big claim to fame. It's exciting to think that God might use you to share the gospel with such a high-profile convert. A pastor's connection to the celebrity can make the pastor a minicelebrity too. Adam Tyson, pastor of a small church in California, reportedly met with Kanye West for personal Bible study over a few months. Tyson admonished West that his Sunday Services weren't really church. After that, West invited Tyson to preach at two of his concerts. At that point, Tyson swapped his Sunday suit for skinny jeans.[16]

Brand Ambassadors

No narrative has more defined white evangelicals in the US over the past half century than embattlement—the "holy war" that Falwell warned of. To be a Christian is to understand yourself as not of the world, as someone whom the world hates. The more you are reviled and marginalized, the stronger and purer your faith will be.

In one way, embattlement is inherent to the faith. The late Anglican theologian John Stott noted that "persecution is simply the clash between two irreconcilable value systems."[17] Jesus told his followers to expect war, suffering, and revilement. After all, "'a servant is not greater than his master.' If they persecuted me, they will persecute you also" (John 15:20). Likewise, John the Evangelist taught the early Christians not to be surprised that the world hates them (1 John 3:13). Paul said that "everyone who wants to live a godly life in Christ Jesus will be persecuted" (2 Tim. 3:12). Stories of martyrdom, today and in ages past, witness to the cost of proclaiming Christ's name in a hostile world.

Yet in a relatively comfortable place and time like ours, persecution narratives are absorbed into the broader, all-consuming culture wars of the past half century. Unlike Christians around the globe, white evangelicals in the US do not face threats of death *because* of their faith. (The story is different for black Christians. Recall the martyrdom of the four black girls killed at the 16th Street Baptist Church bombing in 1963, and the nine killed at Emanuel African Methodist Episcopal Church in 2015. In these and other grievous tragedies, black Americans were killed because they claimed Jesus as their own. White supremacists don't like a Jesus who wants to set black Americans free.) Even still, many evangelicals understandably believe they could lose their job, social standing, or church building with any new administration or legal ruling. Threats from without are seen as evidence of true faith within.

Politicians and media have capitalized on this sense of embattlement. In the late 1970s and early '80s, Falwell, Paul Weyrich, and other political strategists used it to mobilize a powerful voting bloc whose effects were still felt in the 2016 and 2020 elections. Today, news pundits and advocacy groups frame local skirmishes as a war that Christians are about to lose (unless they support the right candidates, of course). The War on Christmas doesn't really exist, but in its ability to stoke fear and ire, it really *works*.

Sensationalized stories of persecution are successful in part because they tell many Christians what they want to hear. As Alan Noble writes, "Being a 'loser' in the world's eyes for the sake of Jesus [is], paradoxically, cool."[18] I learned as a teenager that I should aspire to be a Jesus Freak, to be "othered" by peers, to stand out for faith. If I wasn't a freak, then I was conforming to secular standards. Today, the popular *God's Not Dead* movies envision a Christian college student being forced to sign a statement that God is, in fact, dead, or pastors being forced to turn their sermon notes over to the government. The stories are very literal—no professor would force a student to sign a paper with the words "God is dead" on it—and hackneyed. "They fetishize suffering," writes Noble.[19] But they're popular because they bluntly tap into white Christians' fears of where America is headed.

Jesus *did* tell his followers to be different. Christians are the light of the world, the salt of the earth. They shine their light before others. They are different from their neighbors. The Beatitudes describe this countercultural witness. Yes, many of our neighbors might reject us. But just because someone rejects Christian beliefs doesn't make Christians victims of intolerance. It certainly doesn't amount to persecution. Living in a pluralistic society means living among people who believe differently from you and who may reject your most cherished, core beliefs. And living as Christians means loving them. As Stott said about persecution, "We are not to retaliate like an unbeliever, nor to sulk like a child, nor to lick our wounds in self-pity like a dog."[20] In a word, we are to face it all with *joy*.

Even still, the past forty years have left many Christians sensing they no longer sit at the head of cultural and political power. They're not even sure they have a seat at the table anymore. They certainly can't assume their neighbors (or national leaders) treat Christian faith as normative. Over time, "believers can come to see victimhood as part of their identity."[21]

An overwhelming sense of losing power leads many Christians to align with strongmen—individuals who will represent and defend the faith in high places. In politics, this has obviously meant supporting leaders who promise to uphold Christians' moral concerns or defend their rights to worship and to conduct their affairs according to conscience. In the realms of the arts, entertainment, and mass media, this means Christians are eager to embrace famous people who will represent the faith well in a hostile culture.

Instead of critiquing celebrity culture, and the prevailing power of individuals over institutions in our time, we've simply adopted it, hoping to find a celebrity icon in our likeness. In a time when church attendance and affiliation are declining, Christians hope representatives with megaplatforms might turn the tide. This explains why some megachurch pastors have cozied up with pop star Justin Bieber, who regularly speaks of his faith in Christ. When Bieber posts positively about his pastor friends, or the Bible, or his marriage, he lends legitimacy to a faith we fear our neighbors see as stodgy or bigoted. Allie Jones notes that Bieber's public ties to the church have "done for Pentecostal megachurches what Tom Cruise did for Scientology and Madonna did for Kabbalah."[22] He's a good spokesman for the Christian brand.

In this way, evangelicals' embrace of Kanye West wasn't merely about the artistry of *Jesus Is King*. West's conversion was a culturally symbolic win, a tally on the Christian side, over against the scores of secular artists who embrace ungodly values. Even Focus on the Family praised *Jesus Is King*—not because of its artistic merits, to be clear. Rather, the reviewer was excited that West's conversion might rub off on Kardashian and change the way she dresses:

> How incredible would it be for one of the most famous women in the world, who's known to wear extremely revealing clothing, to change her mind and adopt a more modest style as an expression of her newfound faith.[23]

If Kardashian accepted Christ alongside her then husband, who could really deny the credibility of Christianity or its teachings on modesty? The power of the kingdom of Kimye, with a combined estimated net worth of $2.1 billion, cannot be denied.[24] If the entire Kimye kingdom were converted to Christianity, Christians would have a foothold of power in a hostile world. (Sadly, the Kimye kingdom appears to be crumbling; West and Kardashian are set to divorce at the time of this writing.)

For his part, West explicitly acknowledged he was God's spokesperson. On *The Late Late Show* in 2019, he said:

> God is using me as a human being. . . . As humbly as I can put it, he's using me to show off. Last year, I made $115 million and still ended up $35 million in debt. This year, I looked up and I just got $68 million returned to me on my tax returns. And people say, "Oh, don't talk about these numbers." No,

people need to hear someone that's been put into debt by the system talk about these kind of numbers now that they're in service to Christ.[25]

West—as humbly as he can put it—saw his handsome tax returns as evidence of God's favor. Christ would make him not only famous but also rich, all for Christ's glory. It's fitting that West has aligned himself with prosperity preacher Joel Osteen and former president Donald Trump, who regularly boasts about his alleged millions. For these and other uniquely American icons, wealth and fame are signs of unique blessing and power. They are attractive to people who feel culturally marginalized and face systemic injustice or simply the difficulties of life. Where we feel weak, they are strong.

Evangelicals, who feel uniquely disempowered by cultural shifts of the past fifty years, inordinately celebrate these celebrity conversions. "We celebrate a conversion because *it says something about the legitimacy of what we believe*. We don't feel so 'out there' or so 'strange' when a respected celebrity gives us a nod. . . . Because the world says celebrities 'count more,' we think their conversion counts more, too."[26]

Make Christianity Cool Again

As much as evangelicals believe they should be different from the world, they also want to be part of it. This is part of the evangelical ethos, going back at least to the 1940s, after they had split from their separatist cousins in the great modernist-fundamentalist divide. Evangelicals maintain the authority of Scripture, the necessity of conversion, and the historic creeds. In this way, they hold fast to the "fundamentals" and reject modernists' cultural accommodation, especially on how to read Scripture in light of modern scientific findings and shifts in sexual ethics.

Unlike fundamentalists, however, evangelicals are eager to engage the social issues of the day, to show that Christianity is relevant to all dimensions of modern life and thought. If you've ever heard the phrase "in the world but not of it," you get the twin polarities of evangelical consciousness. You want to be both separate *and* respected, if not always entirely accepted.

Being "in the world but not of it" has produced some odd outcomes. A hallmark of many evangelical upbringings was swapping out secular CDs for their Christian counterparts. Bye Alanis Morissette, hello Rebecca St. James. At the time, there was great satisfaction in recognizing that Rebecca was just as cool—well, almost as cool—as Alanis. Being a Christian didn't mean you had to give up *taste* or edginess, an important factor for a teenager in public high school. I could listen to confessional lyrics that sounded like top 40 radio instead of hymns. I'll never forget how triumphant I felt telling my high school boyfriend, the aforementioned atheist, that the punk band MxPx was Christian. (To be fair, their explicit faith content was more prevalent on earlier records, when they were with indie label Tooth & Nail.) He looked horrified, and I felt giddy: an *atheist* had been listening to Christians without even knowing it. Gotcha!

The seeker-sensitive church movement grew out of a desire to be both evangelistic and culturally relevant. When my Methodist church played movie clips during Sunday worship, we were signaling to visitors that we, too, enjoyed Hollywood blockbusters. (This many years later, I'm still fuzzy on how *The Polar Express* captures the gospel.) Willow Creek's Global Leadership

Summit demonstrates that Christians could be on the cutting edge of leadership and organizational innovation. One needn't leave intelligence or style at the doors of the church.

Likewise, the "hipster Christianity" trend that Brett McCracken wrote about in 2010. Rebelling against the evangelical kitsch of their upbringing, younger Christians wanted to show their peers that Christians could cuss, have tattoos, watch R-rated movies, and enjoy good coffee and Belgian Tripels.[27] They had traded in the anthem rock of U2 (now playing at their parents' suburban megachurch) for ancient hymns. It's not clear to me whether hipster Christianity is (1) still a thing and (2) an attempt at cultural relevance, or Christians simply being young people who live in cities. Even still, hipster-friendly churches certainly hope to convey that not all Christians are dorks. (Unless you're going for an ironic dorky aesthetic.)

Today, cool churches use luxury clothing, well-produced music, and celebrity friends to attract millennials and Gen Zers who'd otherwise avoid traditional church. Zoe Church in Los Angeles, Vous Church in Miami, Churchome in Washington State, and Hillsong campuses across the globe use cutting-edge design to make church feel like a nightclub. "It used to be that to be an evangelical Christian was to be like Kirk Cameron or Jeff Foxworthy, old and irrelevant and consigned to made-for-TV B-movies," writes Laura Turner. "But there is an effort from churches like Zoe and Hillsong underway—probably more unconscious than deliberate—to make Christianity accessible, cool, and interesting to young people."[28]

Of course, you're probably more familiar with the pastors' names—and the names of their celebrity friends—than the names of the churches. Chad Veach at Zoe pastors megawatt actor Chris Pratt and wife Katherine Schwarzenegger. Judah

Smith at Churchome is chaplain for the Seattle Seahawks and counts Russell Wilson and pop singer Ciara Wilson as attendees. Rich Wilkerson Jr. at Vous officiated West and Kardashian's wedding. And Carl Lentz, formerly of Hillsong NYC, pastored Selena Gomez, Kevin Durant, Nick Jonas, and Kylie Jenner. All of these pastors have Pentecostal roots. If they have a patron saint, it is Justin Bieber.

Bieber, the Grammy-winning singer with more than 200 million Instagram followers, captures evangelicals' desire to recruit spokespeople for cool Christianity. A Canadian who became a teen idol at fourteen, Bieber speaks openly and regularly about Jesus. In a now-iconic profile of Hillsong Church, journalist Taffy Brodesser-Akner recounts a classic born-again story: Bieber, going through a difficult season sometime around 2010, called his friend Lentz, sobbing. After they prayed together, Bieber was gripped by the reality of God's love and asked to be baptized that night. So Lentz called his friend, former Knicks player Tyson Chandler, and asked if they could use the bathtub of his large Upper West Side home.[29] As Bieber emerged from the NBA player's bathtub, he dedicated his life to Christ. He and his wife, model Hailey Baldwin, were baptized (again) together in 2020 and openly credit Jesus as the center of their marriage.[30]

A 2018 Instagram photo of a shirtless, heavily tattooed Bieber, looking down at an open Bible in his lap, with the caption "wowzers," got more than 8 million likes.[31] There is something truly rare about genuine faith broadcast at that level, by someone with that much cultural cachet. In a celebrity-focused age, it makes sense for ordinary Christians to hope that Bieber's embrace of their faith could rejigger some fans' plausibility structures. No, an Instagram post is unlikely to get many people to church. But it might make them rethink the Christian "brand." If young people want to retain their cool, and if they see from Bieber, Baldwin, West, and others that Christians are on the cutting edge of cool, maybe they will give it another look.

Then again, looking to any celebrity to represent the faith comes with the risk of them representing the faith poorly. There's always the chance that they will renounce the faith or otherwise give it a bad rap. West, for his part, has raised eyebrows for his ties to Trump (with whom he claims to share "dragon energy") as well as for the comment that the four hundred years of chattel slavery in America "sounds like a choice."[32] Bob Dylan stopped writing confessional lyrics and preaching on tour decades ago. The Jonas Brothers ditched their purity rings as they left their squeaky-clean image behind. Besides, plenty of Hollywood actors and pop musicians who claim Christian faith would not neatly fit within the ethical strictures of white evangelicalism (by doing nude scenes, for example, or divorcing and remarrying). If evangelicals are looking for a brand ambassador who will speak and live out their faith in exactly the same way they do, they're going to be disappointed.

Grace is needed for any celebrity working out their faith under the glare of the spotlight. New converts are bound to make mistakes as they grow in the faith. Yet in a reversal of what we might expect, it was Bieber who had to distance himself from his pastor, instead of the pastor distancing himself from a pop star and former bad boy. After Lentz's infidelity came to light, Bieber announced that he no longer attends Hillsong, having switched to Churchome. He and Baldwin unfollowed Lentz on Instagram—a digital excommunication of epic proportions.[33] It was Bieber who came out of the mess looking like the spiritually grounded leader. In early 2021, he told *GQ*,

I think so many pastors put themselves on this pedestal. And it's basically, church can be surrounded around the man, the pastor, the guy, and it's like, "*This* guy has this ultimate relationship with God that we all want but we can't get because we're not *this* guy." That's not the reality, though. The reality is, every human being has the same access to God.[34]

Besides, what makes Christians think the faith is about being cool? In a way, hoping to align with Hollywood Christians is another way for evangelicals to amass power. If the religious right aligned itself with powerful politicians to protect the faith in the halls of Congress, then evangelical leaders aligning with celebrity Christians is a grasping for "the soft power of Hollywood."[35] By now we've seen the wreckage left by the religious right's efforts: alliances with morally bankrupt politicians, a compromised public witness, and a generation of millennials who feel betrayed by their parents' generation and want nothing to do with their faith.

The next generation of church leaders is better off abandoning the fixation on cultural credibility, instead pursuing ordinary faithfulness. Before we hope to convince those outside the house of faith that we are relevant, we need to clean up the house from within.

8

The Obscure Messiah and Ordinary Faithfulness

When I survey the panoply of Christian figures of my teenage faith, I feel so old. Not just because the low-rise jeans that were so popular at the time no longer fit (#momjeansforlife). Not just because my taste in music and movies has matured over twenty years (although I will always enjoy DC Talk's *Jesus Freak*). The primary reason I feel old is that so many of the famous musicians, speakers, pastors, and authors who defined the evangelical movement of my youth have faded from glory. Some have simply stepped out of the limelight, choosing to invest in family or an ordinary career. Some, such as Joshua Harris and Hawk Nelson lead singer Jonathan Steingard, have publicly renounced the faith. Others, like Ravi Zacharias, have proved to be the opposite of the admirable leaders we thought they were. White evangelical culture of the late 1990s, with its WWJD bracelets, Thomas Kinkade paintings, and the Newsboys' revolving drum set, feels like a lifetime ago.

Since that time, a lot of my age peers have left the faith too. For some, Christianity never went deeper than a brand identity. Once the complexities of life, doubt, and suffering hit, the faith as it was taught seemed shallow, something to switch out for something sturdier. Others followed their former role models out the church doors. If one's faith could be sealed by a particular celebrity, it makes sense that it could also be capsized by one too. Others have endured abuse of many forms at the hands of Christian institutions and their leaders. Still others hold fast to Jesus but want nothing to do with the racial, cultural, and political dimensions of white American evangelicalism. Deconversion and "faith detox" are trending topics among my generation.

In light of this, I sometimes wonder why I am still a Christian. What was it about that early faith, especially with its silly youth group trappings, that could blossom into an orientation that could withstand doubt, the loss of dreams, and cultural pressures? Of course, faith is a gift of grace (Eph. 2:8–10). There's nothing I or my parents or youth pastor or Geoff Moore and the Distance or Rebecca St. James could have done or not done apart from the work of God in Christ to make me stay. I approach most days with the acute sense that Christianity has chosen me, rather than the other way around.

Even still, if I could point to a defining factor that has made Christian faith alluring, plausible, and *real* to me, it is this: other Christians. Not specific leaders or figureheads, teaching and preaching from a stage or a screen far away. Certainly not any famous Bible teachers and social media influencers, even the ones whose writing and teaching has undeniably enriched my life. I mean ordinary, flawed, messy fellow humans, working out what it means to love God and neighbor, day in and day out, without fanfare or praise.

I don't even mean people doing "lifestyle evangelism." The people I have in mind don't have their sights set on any strategy, plan, or outcome. Their left hand knows not what their right hand is doing. They simply find their lives taken up in an eternal reality larger than themselves, and they live with a sense that small acts of love in this life carry a great significance in the next.

What makes Christianity—more specifically, Christ—real to me are the people in my life who are living icons.

The word "icon" is from the Greek *eikōn*, meaning "likeness" or "image." All humans bear the image of God. All humans, under the power of sin, also mar the image of God, in themselves and others. And all humans redeemed in Christ— "the image of the invisible God, the firstborn over all creation" (Col. 1:15)—are being restored to their intended brilliance. God is making all things new (Rev. 21:5), and God's great plan of restoration begins with us.

In their traditional usage, icons are artistic renderings of people who have imaged Christ with a particular brilliance. In Eastern Orthodox and some Western traditions, gazing on a painting of a biblical figure or a saint can aid in worship. The physical object is not worshiped; rather, the object is used to focus one's attention on Christ and the life of the world to come.

It's unlikely that evangelicals will take up icons as part of their devotional practice any time soon. But it is good and fitting to honor people, both past and present, for imaging Christ well. The people in my own life who do this don't think of themselves as icons, of course. God's hidden work in their lives is just that—hidden. Most of the time, they are acutely aware of how they fall short of brilliance, how slowly the inner work of transformation seems to unfold. Year after year, they might wonder if they are growing, given that the habits of pride or anger or indulgence keep hanging on. But it's often the case that we can more easily see the goodness in others than we can see it in ourselves. I am so grateful for the goodness I see in them.

I think, first, of my parents, the frugal midwesterners I introduced in chapter 4. Tim and Karen Beaty have been married for forty-plus years, have lived in the same three-bedroom ranch for thirty-plus years, and have belonged to the Methodist church community that I grew up in for twenty-five-plus years. It goes without saying that they are people who stay for the long haul, despite challenges and frustrations (some of which I am aware of and many more I am not). They show me the gift of faithfulness.

I think, too, of the pastor whose Chicago-area church I belonged to as a young adult, who modeled what it looks like to hold Christian conviction with gentleness instead of rancor. I think of a friend who has kept her heart open to the possibility of a child when foreclosing on hope might feel safer. I think of another friend who was plunged into the dark waters of grief after the untimely death of her husband, yet who still exudes joy when no one would blame her for being anything but. Still another friend is simply generous with her attention in conversations, eager to invite more people in, acutely aware of who might be left out and need connection. Another friend found the church to be a safe haven during a traumatic childhood and now pastors a church, leading it to care for the traumatized and marginalized.

These and other people make Christ real to me—not through dramatic or flashy displays that earn praise or attention or get posted on social media. The reality of their faith is forged over the long haul, in mundane acts, choices, and postures of the heart, day in and day out. Strung together, these acts form the content of their lives and the Christian life. Indeed, this is what the Christian life is like for the majority of us, and what it has been for almost all believers for the past two thousand years. The sum witness of all the saints is now barely known to us. It is hidden. And that's how holiness was intended to be. The moment we try to project it out for recognition or credibility, holiness loses some of its brilliance.

The whole apparatus of the church exists to make us holy, to make us like "little Christs." Making "little Christs" (a term often attributed to Luther) is the point of discipleship. C. S. Lewis writes in *Mere Christianity*,

> The Church exists for nothing else but to draw men into Christ, to make them little Christs. If they are not doing that, all the cathedrals, clergy, missions, sermons, even the Bible itself are simply a waste of time. God became Man for no other purpose. It is even doubtful, you know, whether the whole universe was created for any other purpose.[1]

According to Lewis, the church doesn't exist to grow in buildings, budgets, and butts (seats in the pews). It doesn't exist to prove that Christianity is cool, credible, or naturally attractive. It exists to make its people into little Christs. The growth mindset that pervades much of the American church has arguably distracted us from the main thing. Growth in size has often supplanted growth in holiness—and this emphasis has over time subtly justified whatever means might "work" to achieve that growth, with celebrity near the top of the list of strategies.

But what if God would rather have a smaller church composed of persons growing year by year into the likeness of Christ than all the megachurches in the world filled with people who are there to be entertained or to have their felt needs met? Would *we* be able to accept a smaller but more spiritually vibrant church?

Readers hoping the final chapter of this book will offer a solution to the problem of celebrity—or at least a solution that is programmatic and easily implemented—will be disappointed and perhaps a bit annoyed. *Gosh, what a negative book! Are you just going to complain about the problem without trying to fix it?* To be sure, I have hinted throughout this book at some attitudes and practices that could curtail the worst effects of social power without proximity. I have underscored the necessity of structures of accountability in every church and organization and for every leader. I have implied that Christian leaders should get comfortable with going off the grid, getting out of the spotlight, and asking for honest feedback from friends and colleagues. I have called Christian book publishers and authors to a standard higher than the Almighty Dollar. It's probably not a bad idea for anyone entering professional ministry to undergo psychological testing. I trust that some of what I've written and reported on will spark ideas among you, readers, for how to address celebrity in your particular context.

But if we are looking to address celebrity with a solution that can be packaged, sold, and implemented across various channels—especially one that will unwittingly make me or any other teacher a celebrity!—we are back to where we started. If we think we can curtail celebrity's toxic effects with strategy, planning, and effort, we reveal the extent to which we've embraced worldly myths about our own agency and control. The problem of celebrity will not be fixed in any programmatic way. There will be no BuzzFeed-like articles titled "Here Are 10 Weird Tricks to Fix Celebrity, Which Reveals the Propensity of the Human Heart to Create Idols and Abuse Power." The moment we try to "manage" celebrity, we've become like Bilbo Baggins. If we think we can slip on the ring from time to time, using it only when necessary or when it serves a greater good, we miss how it is changing us into someone, or something, else that is terrifying and inhuman.

We can't program our way out of this one. There is no program for addressing the problem of celebrity. There is only a Person. And he, thankfully, knew exactly what it was like to wrestle with the temptation of worldly power.

The Temptation to Power

Jesus of Nazareth is the most famous person to have ever lived. In two millennia, the spiritual community founded in his name has become the world's largest. Christianity started as a small sect of Judaism in the first century. Today, it claims more than 30 percent of the world's 7.3 billion people.[2]

Orthodox theologian Jaroslav Pelikan writes that Jesus "has been the most dominant figure in the history of Western culture for almost twenty centuries. If it were possible, with some sort of super magnet, to pull up out of that history every scrap of metal bearing at least a trace of his name, how much would be left?"[3] In different cultural contexts, Pelikan writes, Jesus has been embraced as Rabbi, King of kings, the Light of the Gentiles, the Liberator, and the Prince of Peace, depending on the cultural milieu in different times and places. Dallas Willard writes in *The Divine Conspiracy*:

> Today, from countless paintings, statues, and buildings, from literature and history, from personality and institution, from profanity, popular song, and entertainment media, from confession and controversy, from legend and ritual—Jesus stands quietly at the center of the contemporary world, as he himself predicted.[4]

Nothing about Jesus's earthly life would have anticipated this legacy. He had inauspicious beginnings. He was born in a stable to a teenage mother and an overwhelmed carpenter father. Nazareth was a minor village in the backwaters of Galilee, which was a minor region in the backwaters of the Roman Empire. Israel was on the fringe of a vast empire. And Jesus looked nothing like its rulers.

He spent the first thirty years of his life outside public ministry. After his father died, notes Willard, Jesus became a carpenter, a blue-collar worker. Scripture says that "he had no beauty or majesty to attract us to him, nothing in his appearance that we should desire him" (Isa. 53:2). The fact that his features aren't mentioned in the Gospels suggests that they were unremarkable. When he entered into public ministry, he didn't start in the seat of cultural and political power. Rather, he started in Capernaum and Bethsaida, "the farthest outposts of Jewish life in the Palestine of his day," rather than the "bright lights of Jerusalem."[5]

Even there, the names of Caesar Augustus and Tiberius Caesar would have loomed large. Augustus was the Roman emperor when Jesus was born. His military power was mighty enough to disrupt Jesus's preborn life, when he decreed that a census be taken of the Roman world, forcing Mary and Joseph to travel to Bethlehem. When Augustus died, he was worshiped as a god, just as his great-uncle, Julius Caesar, had been. Tiberius Caesar, who ruled during most of Jesus's life and ministry, had godlike stature as well. His likeness appeared on many coins (denarii) used throughout the empire. The denarii made him a kind of protocelebrity, taking his image far beyond the physical confines of the imperial palace.

Every coin of the empire reminded citizens to whom they owed allegiance. This was a political claim and a spiritual one as well. Despite the crowds that were gathering around Jesus and his disciples, it's unlikely Caesar would have known about Jesus. But Jesus knew about Caesar and his expansive, godlike power. Which is why it was alarming when he implied that Caesar is *not* God—that Caesar's power is of this world and thus will be returned to him. As Andy Crouch writes, paraphrasing Mark 12:17, "Render back to Caesar the coin of his realm . . . and render to God whatever, or whoever, bears his image."[6] Let Caesar have his dominion, because it is fleeting anyway.

Even still, Jesus could imagine what Caesar's type of power could do—how it might even be wielded for godly purposes. That's one of the great temptations of power: to think that it can be used as a tool without it shaping and eventually disfiguring us in the process. Jesus knew this temptation firsthand. Before entering public ministry, he went alone to the desert to fast and pray. There, taking advantage of Jesus's weakness and isolation, Satan appeared to him three times. He tempted Jesus to turn stones into bread, to jump from the temple, and to bow down to him in exchange for all the kingdoms of the world.

One way to think about these three temptations is to see them as ways Jesus could have claimed a power apart from the plans of God. Henri Nouwen, the Catholic writer whom we met in chapter 6, summarizes them as the three temptations of a Christian leader:

1. The temptation to be *relevant*. By turning stones into bread, Jesus is tempted not only to provide for himself but also to "do something that makes people realize that we do make a difference in their lives."

2. The temptation to be *spectacular*. By flinging himself off the highest point of the temple and asking angels to save him, Jesus is tempted to "draw thousands of people" like a magician or stuntman who wows and entertains a crowd.

3. The temptation to be *powerful*. By bowing to Satan, Jesus is tempted to rule over the kingdoms of the world in their splendor. Notably, Nouwen writes, the temptation to power "is greatest when intimacy is a threat. Much Christian leadership is exercised by people who do not know how to develop healthy, intimate relationships and have opted for power and control instead."[7]

Fully God and fully man, Jesus empathizes with our draw to seek worldly power—to adopt the mechanisms and metrics of the world to fulfill kingdom purposes. He has been tempted in every way we have been (Heb. 4:15)—yet he chose the better path. Eugene Peterson notes in his book *The Jesus Way* that the Son of God would have found this last temptation particularly strong, because he was the *most* qualified person to run the world:

What an offer! Who is more qualified? Here is the opportunity to establish a rule of peace and justice and prosperity. Create a government free of corruption. But of course it would have to be on the devil's terms, a rule conditioned by the unholy *if*—"if you will fall down and worship me." The devil's way would be absolutely perfect in its functions, but with no personal relationships.[8]

Peterson summarizes Jesus's testing in the desert: "In the three great refusals, Jesus refuses to do good things in the wrong way."[9] Feeding people, evangelizing by miracles, and ruling the world justly are all good in and of themselves. But Jesus's refusal to give in tells us that we can't do good things in bad ways and expect the ends to justify the means. *How* we do kingdom things matters. Obedience to God's ways of bringing about the kingdom is the only way, even when those ways seem small, obscure, and weak. Even when no one notices. Even when our kingdom work can't be captured and packaged for a ready-made inspirational social media update. Someone earnestly desiring to do great things for God can have all the right motives but all the wrong mechanisms. Jesus's obedience tells us that mechanisms matter—if godly ends are pursued by ungodly means, the whole project will be ruined.

As an antidote to the temptation to worldly power, Jesus frequently chose obscurity. He entered ministry late in the game, "wasting" his immense gifts and education working as a carpenter. He was followed by crowds yet often went away to be alone. He was seen in public with people who would have sullied his social standing: prostitutes, tax collectors, people with diseases and disabilities. His disciples were a ragtag bunch, not particularly impressive or alluring. And who could imagine a more obscure, ignoble death? Jesus was abandoned by his dearest friends, falsely tried, mocked, whipped, and finally hung on a tree between two criminals. How overwhelming the temptation must have been in those final, brutal hours to take matters into his own hands, to respond to the power of the unjust rulers and sneering crowds with his own, far superior power. Instead, by submitting to God's will, "he humbled himself by becoming obedient to death—even death on a cross!" (Phil. 2:8).

After the crucifixion, his ministry might have looked like a failure—what an absurd way for a life to end. The disciples were sad and scared, perhaps a bit embarrassed that their spiritual leader was killed, their spiritual project all for naught. Yet, through the way of the cross, God "exalted him to the highest place and gave him the name that is above every name, that at the name of Jesus every knee should bow, in heaven and on earth and under the earth, and every tongue acknowledge that Jesus Christ is Lord, to the glory of God the Father" (Phil. 2:9–11). The power to rule all things justly *was* granted to the resurrected Jesus, but only after he obeyed the mysterious, upside-down ways of God.

Celebrity, in the final analysis, is a worldly form of power and evaluation of human worth. It is not a spiritually neutral tool that can be picked up and put down, even for godly projects. The moment celebrity is adopted and adapted for otherwise noble purposes—sharing the good news and inviting others into rich kingdom life—it changes the project. And it changes us.

In a time when large swaths of the American church have merely mimicked worldly concepts of power, going for bigger, louder, and glitzier, we have to return to the small, the quiet, the uncool, and the ordinary. Obscurity may very well be the spiritual discipline the American church needs to practice the most in the coming century. In order to detox from the effects of celebrity in our midst and preserve Christianity's countercultural understanding of power, we must recapture a vision of ordinary faithfulness, a vision of the Christian life that begins and ends with producing "little Christs." In all of this, we must practice *proximity*—valuing flesh-and-blood relationships over mediated ones, choosing intimacy over fandom, and letting others into the real contours of our behind-the-scenes lives, where our vulnerabilities and weaknesses are on display. The only way to follow Christ is together, walking side by side toward "the life that is truly life" (1 Tim. 6:19).

In order to go up, we have to go low—uncomfortably low. That's how it worked for Jesus, the Son of God. "He had a different way of using power in the world, a way that turned out to outlast all the emperors, including the Christian ones," notes Crouch.[10] What makes us, Jesus's disciples, think we could do it any other way?

A Hidden Life

None of this is new. I'm glad to have nothing novel to offer to address the problem of celebrity. (I will not be repackaging this book into a downloadable celebrity detox starter pack.) For decades, each in their own way, writers like Eugene Peterson, Dallas Willard, Richard Foster, Ruth Haley Barton, and Henri Nouwen have called us to embrace a Christian life of integrity, humility, and simplicity. And none of them were reinventing the wheel. They were simply mining and gifting us with the riches of the Christian tradition, applying the wisdom of Augustine of Hippo, Saints Felicitas and Perpetua, Ignatius of Loyola, Teresa of Ávila, François Fénelon, Dietrich Bonhoeffer, Howard Thurman, and Thomas Merton, among many others, to our frenetic and fractured age.

These have been like voices crying in the wilderness, calling the American church out of the trappings of size, spectacle, and sensationalism to a life of ordinary faithfulness in our individual and corporate lives. They've called Christian leaders back to the primary vocation to shepherd souls, which requires an intimacy and knowledge that the church growth movement has largely precluded. And even while these prophets published books, received awards and speaking invitations, and are now household names among evangelicals, they have largely resisted attention-seeking via mass media, cultivating a curated brand, or pursuing a lavish lifestyle. Few of us could do the same.

But surely we could have been paying better attention to them when they were sounding the alarm on the church's coziness with celebrity. Maybe they aren't prophets crying out in the wilderness. They're on our bookshelves and quoted in our sermons, after all. We just didn't want to listen to them.

Reflecting on *The Rise and Fall of Mars Hill* podcast, Andy Crouch told me in an interview that

> at the very moment that Mark Driscoll was going from strength to strength and outrage to outrage . . . we had Eugene Peterson writing about pastoring, we had Dallas Willard writing and speaking and teaching. . . . You had this alternate account of faithful leadership, and it's not like it was totally dead in the water. Eugene Peterson was very well known in the '90s and aughts. Willard's books sold just fine. These were people who made millions of dollars publishing books that evangelicals read. It's not like they were marginal.
>
> And yet in the end, it just didn't matter much. Here was this other beautiful thing, men of true integrity, . . . and too many of us just didn't want it. In the end, that's not what we wanted to buy or install as our representatives. It's like we got Peter

and Paul, and then we got Simon the Magician, and we're like, "Thank you, we'll take Simon."[11]

Simon, in case you forgot who he is (as I had!), is mentioned briefly in Acts. He drew crowds and praise by practicing sorcery. He was his own hype man, boasting that "he was someone great" (8:9). People called him "the Great Power of God" and followed him wherever he went. Then he heard the gospel preached by Philip, turned to Christ, and was baptized. He watched signs and miracles performed by Philip through the real power of God instead of the false power of magic. He wanted that kind of power but mistakenly thought he could buy it for his own gain. When he offered to purchase it from Peter and John, they harshly rebuked him.

Perhaps large swaths of the American church prefer our Simons over Philips because we don't believe that the gospel, lived out daily in ordinary, embedded community, will be enough to captivate our neighbors, especially in a time when many of them have walked away from the church or simply don't see it as relevant to their lives. Perhaps we're anxious that, unless we play by the world's rules for what counts as success, we'll lose. We have the right message, but like Simon trying to shore up crowds with spectacle, we use the modern wizardries of digital technology to entertain and entrance. We amplify our platforms, projecting images of our favorite teachers on screens, hoping their charisma, folksy humor, and good looks will attract crowds. Sure, maybe some people will come for the wrong reasons, but eventually we can convert them into disciples— right? To be sure, screens are not inherently evil, nor are large churches, social media platforms, or charismatic personalities. But if we keep leaning on these strategies and techniques that simply mimic the worlds of entertainment and celebrity worship, we shouldn't be surprised that we draw crowds who are more interested in the celebrity than the Christ to whom they're trying to point.

I asked Crouch what people with some measure of celebrity power can do to limit it. I imagine that a few readers of this book are legit celebrities and sincerely hope to steward it well, without becoming monks or hermits or walking away from their calling entirely (although on the whole I think anyone in Christian leadership should commit to seasons of obscurity). They believe God has given them a platform and don't want to use it for the wrong reasons.

I have grappled with my own limited celebrity too. It's easy for me to think of other Christians with much larger public profiles and conclude that, because mine is small in comparison, I'm off the hook. But I've spoken to audiences, had my face and voice projected on screens, and participated in the book publishing industry. My face has been on TV (that was super weird), and my words have appeared in national print media (that was more fun). I've felt pressure to grow my social media following (especially in preparation for launching a book!). In truth, many more readers than would acknowledge it participate in the economy of celebrity on some level. If people follow you on social media, you're at least swimming in celebrity waters.

I was struck by the simplicity of what Crouch told me: friendship. None of us need another fan. We all need another friend. "We're meant to have people in our lives who are so close to us that nothing can impress them and nothing can shock them," he told me in our interview. This is another description of *proximity*—the antidote to celebrity's isolating effects. Proximity happens when we are fully known and fully loved, which is the thing all of us, celebrity or not, are made for.

Anyone who's had a friend tell them the honest truth knows that this proximity is not always fun. It's not for the faint of heart. It requires a commitment to show up for each other—if we are lucky, until the end of our earthly lives. It's not transactional or mutual back-scratching as a means to the goal of fame. It's not entered into with the expectation that you'll endorse each other's books or that they'll post that cute photo of you together on Instagram where your hair looked especially good. An ideal friend will have known you (and loved you) long before you were famous. Celebrities find it hard to have genuine friends, because once you've made it to the green room or the private jet, "normal people" seem less exciting. They won't propel you to the higher echelon.

It's easier to have a fan than a friend. A fan will only reflect back to you your own simulated glory. A friend, on the other hand, will reflect back to you your true glory. Which is another way of saying that they will remind you, if they are a good friend, of your belovedness in Christ, apart from praise or performance. Your true glory is not in what you do or how many books you sell or how many people listen to your podcast or what people on the internet say about you, but in your inherent, inestimable worth as an image bearer of the Lord of the universe. Your true glory is now seen only dimly but will one day be fully revealed at the redemption of all things (Rom. 8:18). Friends who remind us of our true glory are very rare and very precious.

Maybe this kind of friendship is another way of talking about ordinary faithfulness. Maybe loving each other in this way is the sum of what it means to become "little Christs."

Maybe this is what it means to be stitched together in his living body, binding up each other's wounds, carrying each other's burdens, celebrating each other's joys and successes, serving each other as Christ served us. Maybe this is the greatest evangelistic strategy at our disposal: to love as Christ loved us, seeking to serve rather than be served, in quiet, everyday, unseen ways.

There is one literary figure who captures this hidden faithfulness for me perfectly. Dorothea Brooke, the heroine of George Eliot's 1872 novel *Middlemarch*, begins her adult life with high ideals and the desire to do something spectacular, noble, and brilliant. She aspires to be a Theresa of Ávila of her time, a saint who forsakes the creature comforts of home and family to live "totally on fire for God," to borrow a term from evangelical parlance. She attempts to achieve this, to disastrous effects, by marrying a much older clergyman, whose magnum opus she intends to help him finish. The marriage proves to be joyless and loveless, and after her husband dies, Dorothea's ideals give way to quieter and humbler ways of caring for the people around her: learning to see her late husband's harsh demeanor with compassion, lending money to a friend to cover a sizable debt that has hurt his reputation, and supporting a snobbish, unlikable acquaintance struggling in her marriage. Even after her big, youthful plans have faded, Dorothea finds new meaning in practices of common goodness, an intent to love and seek to understand the people around her. She would not go down in history as her own time's Teresa of Ávila. But her world would be incalculably more tender because of small, everyday acts of kindness.

Here is how Eliot puts it, in one of the most gorgeous finales to a novel imaginable:

[Dorothea's] full nature . . . spent itself in channels which had no great name on the earth. But the effect of her being on those around her was incalculably diffusive: for the growing good of the world is partly dependent on unhistoric acts; and that things are not so ill with you and me as they might have been, is half owing to the number who lived faithfully a hidden life, and rest in unvisited tombs.[12]

Maybe recovering from celebrity's toxic effects means accepting that our lives will be mostly a series of "unhistoric acts" whose final effects remain unknown to the world. Maybe it means casting off the big ideals of living big lives for God and accepting that our greatest moments of faithfulness may be achieved in complete obscurity. Maybe it means getting back down to the roots—to something as small as a mustard seed. To a faith that is hidden and unnoticed, barely visible to the human eye. The kingdom of God is not coming through bright lights and loudspeakers and impressive buildings and multi-media teaching series and PR specialists and strategic partnerships and viral content. It is not coming through entertaining anecdotes and polished talks and bestselling books. It is not coming through any strategy. It's not even coming through you and me. We don't build or usher in the kingdom of God. We merely attest to its reality in our lives. If only we would get out of the way.

Acknowledgments

This book wouldn't exist without my agent, Joy Eggerichs Reed, who became extremely animated when I first mentioned this book idea to her three years ago; my gracious and professional colleagues at Brazos—Jim, Eric, Melisa, Jeremy, Erin, Shelly, Brian, Bob, and Janelle; the friends who have encouraged me along the way, especially Annie, Sarah, Maria, Kate, and Katie; the interview subjects who graciously and vulnerably shared their stories and insights for this book; and my family. Mom, Dad, Nonnie, Ty, Sara, and Luther: thank you for knowing me deeply and loving me all the same.

Notes

Chapter 1: Social Power without Proximity

1. Amy Sherman, *Kingdom Calling: Vocational Stewardship for the Common Good* (Downers Grove, IL: InterVarsity, 2011), 46.

2. "Remembering Rosa Parks," *PBS NewsHour*, October 25, 2005, https://www.pbs.org/newshour/show/remembering-rosa-parks.

3. Megan Garber, "Why Are They 'Stars'?," *Atlantic*, February 24, 2017, https://www.theatlantic.com/entertainment/archive/2017/02/why-are-celebrities-known-as-stars/517674.

4. Daniel J. Boorstin, *The Image: A Guide to Pseudo-Events in America* (1962; repr., New York: Knopf, 2012), 53.

5. Barnaby Lane, "Michael Jordan Has Made $1.3 Billion from His 36-Year Partnership with Nike," *Insider*, May 5, 2020, https://www.insider.com/michael-jordan-nike-billions-wanted-adidas-deal-2020-5.

6. Boorstin, *Image*, 57–58.

7. Chavie Lieber, "How and Why Do Influencers Make So Much Money?," *Vox*, November 28, 2018, https://www.vox.com/the-goods/2018/11/28/18116875/influencer-marketing-social-media-engagement-instagram-youtube.

8. Yalda T. Uhls, cited in Stuart Wolpert, "Popular TV Shows Teach Children Fame Is Most Important Value, UCLA Psychologists Report," UCLA Newsroom, July 11, 2011, https://newsroom.ucla.edu/releases/popular-tv-shows-teach-children-210119.

9. Wolpert, "Popular TV Shows."

10. Dara Greenwood, Christopher R. Long, and Sonya Dal Cin, "Fame and the Social Self: The Need to Belong, Narcissism, and Relatedness Predict

the Appeal of Fame," *Personality and Individual Differences* 55, no. 5 (September 2013): 490–95.

11. Deena Weinstein and Michael Weinstein, "Celebrity Worship as Weak Religion," *Word and World* 23, no. 23 (Summer 2003): 297, 301.

12. Andy Crouch, "It's Time to Reckon with Celebrity Power," The Gospel Coalition, March 24, 2018, https://www.thegospelcoalition.org/article/time -reckon-celebrity-power.

13. Daniel Silliman and Kate Shellnutt, "Ravi Zacharias Hid Hundreds of Pictures of Women, Abuse during Massages, and a Rape Allegation," *Christianity Today*, February 11, 2021, https://www.christianitytoday.com/news/2021 /february/ravi-zacharias-rzim-investigation-sexual-abuse-sexting-rape.html.

Chapter 2: The First Evangelical Celebrities

1. George Marsden, *Understanding Fundamentalism and Evangelicalism* (Grand Rapids: Eerdmans, 1991), 6.

2. The Bebbington quadrilateral identifies four defining convictions and attitudes among evangelicals: *biblicism* (all spiritual knowledge is to be found in the Bible, the authoritative Word of God); *crucicentrism* (Christ's atoning death on the cross is central to salvation); *conversionism* (people need to be converted); and *activism* (the gospel is lived out in all dimensions of life, with effort). David Bebbington, *Evangelicalism in Modern Britain: A History from the 1730s to the 1980s* (London: Routledge, 1989).

3. Timothy Gloege, *Guaranteed Pure: The Moody Bible Institute, Business, and the Making of Modern Evangelicalism* (Chapel Hill: University of North Carolina Press, 2015), 19.

4. Gloege, *Guaranteed Pure*, 40.

5. William Thomas Ellis, *Billy Sunday: The Man and His Message* (Philadelphia: John C. Winston, 1917), 155.

6. "Billy Sunday: Salty Evangelist," *Christianity Today*, accessed January 6, 2022, https://www.christianitytoday.com/history/people /evangelistsandapologists/billy-sunday.html.

7. Bruce J. Evensen, "'It Is a Marvel to Many People': Dwight L. Moody, Mass Media, and the New England Revival of 1877," *New England Quarterly* 72, no. 2 (June 1999): 254.

8. Evensen, "'It Is a Marvel to Many People,'" 259.

9. Gloege, *Guaranteed Pure*, 34.

10. Cecilia Rasmussen, "Billy Graham's Star Was Born at His 1949 Revival in Los Angeles," *Los Angeles Times*, September 2, 2007, https://www.latimes .com/archives/la-xpm-2007-sep-02-me-then2-story.html.

11. Grant Wacker, *America's Pastor: Billy Graham and the Shaping of a Nation* (Cambridge, MA: Belknap, 2014), 81, quoted in Kristin du Mez, *Jesus and John Wayne: How White Evangelicals Corrupted a Faith and Fractured a Nation* (New York: Liveright, 2020), 23.

12. Ed Stetzer, phone interview with the author, March 22, 2021.

13. Mark Ward Sr., "Billy Graham and the Power of Media Celebrity," National Communication Association, March 15, 2018, https://www.natcom.org/communication-currents/billy-graham-and-power-media-celebrity.

14. Billy Graham, quoted in Neil Postman, *Amusing Ourselves to Death: Public Discourse in the Age of Show Business* (New York: Penguin, 1985), 118.

15. Postman, *Amusing Ourselves to Death*, 118.

16. Postman, *Amusing Ourselves to Death*, 118.

17. Grant Wacker, "Billy Graham's America," *Church History* 78, no. 3 (September 2009): 491.

18. Andy Crouch, "It's Time to Reckon with Celebrity Power," The Gospel Coalition, March 24, 2018, https://www.thegospelcoalition.org/article/time-reckon-celebrity-power.

19. Bob Smietana, "The Other Billy Graham Rules," *Christianity Today*, March 31, 2017, https://www.christianitytoday.com/ct/2017/march-web-only/other-billy-graham-rules.html.

20. Crouch, "It's Time to Reckon with Celebrity Power."

21. Yuval Levin, "The Case for Wooden Pews," *Deseret News*, January 18, 2021, https://www.deseret.com/indepth/2021/1/18/21564215/why-hard-religion-is-important-american-faith-yuval-levin-gallup-declining-trust-in-institutions.

22. Yuval Levin, "How Did Americans Lose Faith in Everything?," *New York Times*, January 18, 2020, https://www.nytimes.com/2020/01/18/opinion/sunday/institutions-trust.html.

23. Levin, "How Did Americans Lose Faith in Everything?"

24. Levin, "How Did Americans Lose Faith in Everything?"

Chapter 3: Megachurch, Megapastors

1. Bill Hybels, *Courageous Leadership: Field-Tested Strategy for the 360 Degree Leader* (Grand Rapids: Zondervan, 2002), 27.

2. Hybels, *Courageous Leadership*, 17–18.

3. Robert Schuller, quoted in Anne C. Loveland and Otis B. Wheeler, *From Meetinghouse to Megachurch: A Material and Cultural History* (Columbia: University of Missouri Press, 2003), 119.

4. Warren Bird and Scott Thumma, "Megachurch 2020: The Changing Reality in America's Largest Churches," Hartford Institute for Religion Research, page 2, https://faithcommunitiestoday.org/wp-content/uploads/2020/10/Megachurch-Survey-Report_HIRR_FACT-2020.pdf.

5. Kate Bowler, *The Preacher's Wife: The Precarious Power of Evangelical Women Celebrities* (Princeton: Princeton University Press, 2019), 17.

6. Scott Thumma, "Exploring the Megachurch Phenomena: Their Characteristics and Cultural Context," Hartford Institute for Religion Research, http://hirr.hartsem.edu/bookshelf/thumma_article2.html.

7. Thumma, "Exploring the Megachurch Phenomena."

8. Charity Rakestraw, "Seeking Souls, Selling Salvation: A History of the Modern Megachurch," in *Handbook of Megachurches*, ed. Stephen Hunt (Boston: Brill, 2020), 23–42.

9. Global Leadership Network website (https://globalleadership.org), accessed January 6, 2022.

10. Aimee, interview with the author, June 18, 2021.

11. Laura Barringer, interview with the author, June 4, 2021.

12. Russell Chandler, "'Customer' Poll Shapes a Church," *Los Angeles Times*, December 11, 1989, https://www.latimes.com/archives/la-xpm-1989 -12-11-mn-126-story.html.

13. Haddon Robinson and Craig Brian Larson, *The Art and Craft of Biblical Preaching: A Comprehensive Resource for Today's Communicators* (Grand Rapids: Zondervan, 2005).

14. Hybels, *Courageous Leadership*, 47.

15. Nancy Beach, interview with the author, June 7, 2021.

16. Willow Creek Independent Advisory Group, "IAG Report," February 26, 2019, https://globalleadership.org/wp-content/uploads/2019/02 /IAGReport_022819.pdf.

17. Chandler, "'Customer' Poll Shapes a Church"; Bill Hybels and Lynne Hybels, *Fit to Be Tied: Making Marriage Last a Lifetime* (Grand Rapids: Zondervan, 1997), 163–64.

18. "03-23-18 Willow Response," 44:38–46:56, quoted in Scot McKnight and Laura Barringer, *A Church Called Tov: Forming a Goodness Culture That Resists Abuses of Power and Promotes Healing* (Carol Stream, IL: Tyndale, 2020), 76.

19. McKnight and Barringer, *Church Called Tov*, 77.

20. Tony Merida, "Why Your Church Should Embrace Plural Leadership," The Gospel Coalition, May 7, 2019, https://www.thegospelcoalition .org/article/church-plant-embrace-plural-leadership.

21. James C. Galvin, "Willow Creek Governance Review, 2014–2018," April 14, 2019, page 3, http://web.archive.org/web/20200721185559/https://gallery .mailchimp.com/dfd0f4e0c107728235d2ff080/files/6d3bafc4-0b43-450c-8e1e -4eb1c80771e2/Report_on_Governance_Review_2014_2018_FINAL.pdf.

22. Galvin, "Willow Creek Governance Review," 5.

23. Jerome Socolovsky, "Megachurch Pastor Bill Hybels Resigns, Calls Sexual Accusations 'Flat-Out Lies,'" Religion News Service, April 11, 2018, https://religionnews.com/2018/04/11/megachurch-pastor-bill-hybels-resigns -calls-sexual-accusations-flat-out-lies.

Chapter 4: Abusing Power

1. Jeannie Ortega Law, "Tim Tebow Holds Back Tears in Paying Tribute to His 'Hero of the Faith' Ravi Zacharias," *Christian Post*, May 10, 2020,

https://www.christianpost.com/news/tim-tebow-holds-back-tears-in-paying
-tribute-to-his-hero-of-the-faith-ravi-zacharias.html.

2. Mike Pence (@Mike_Pence), "Deeply saddened to learn of the passing of Ravi Zacharias," Twitter, May 19, 2020, 2:39 p.m., https://twitter.com /mike_pence/status/1262815093580070914.

3. David French, "'You Are One Step Away from Complete and Total Insanity,'" *French Press*, February 14, 2021, https://frenchpress.thedispatch .com/p/you-are-one-step-away-from-complete.

4. Daniel Silliman, "Ravi Zacharias's Ministry Investigates Claims of Sexual Misconduct at Spas," *Christianity Today*, September 29, 2020, https://www.christianitytoday.com/news/2020/september/ravi-zacharias -sexual-harassment-rzim-spa-massage-investiga.html.

5. Daniel Silliman and Kate Shellnutt, "Ravi Zacharias Hid Hundreds of Pictures of Women, Abuse during Massages, and a Rape Allegation," *Christianity Today*, February 11, 2021, https://www.christianitytoday.com/news/2021 /february/ravi-zacharias-rzim-investigation-sexual-abuse-sexting-rape.html.

6. Silliman, "Ravi Zacharias's Ministry Investigates Claims."

7. Katelyn Beaty, "As Willow Creek Reels, Churches Must Reckon with How Power Corrupts," Religion News Service, August 10, 2018, https://religion news.com/2018/08/10/beaty-oped.

8. Andy Crouch, "It's Time to Talk about Power," *Christianity Today*, October 1, 2018, https://www.christianitytoday.com/ct/2013/october/andy -crouch-its-time-to-talk-about-power.html.

9. Theology of Work Project, "Servant Leadership (Matt. 20:20–28)," 2014, https://www.theologyofwork.org/new-testament/matthew/living-in-the -new-kingdom-matthew-18-25/servant-leadership-matthew-2020-28.

10. Mike Cosper, *The Rise and Fall of Mars Hill* (podcast), 2021, https:// www.christianitytoday.com/ct/podcasts/rise-and-fall-of-mars-hill.

11. Wendy Alsup, interview with the author, May 24, 2021.

12. Ruth Moon, "Mark Driscoll Addresses Crude Comments Made Trolling as 'William Wallace II,'" *Christianity Today*, August 1, 2014, https://www .christianitytoday.com/news/2014/august/mark-driscoll-crude-comments -william-wallace-mars-hill.html.

13. Sarah Eekhoff Zylstra, "How Acts 29 Survived—and Thrived—after the Collapse of Mars Hill," The Gospel Coalition, December 5, 2017, https:// www.thegospelcoalition.org/article/how-acts-29-survived-and-thrived-after -the-collapse-of-mars-hill.

14. Scott Thomas, "Happy Birthday and Happy 15th Anniversary, Mark Driscoll," *Acts 29* (blog), October 11, 2011, https://web.archive.org/web /20131112010415/http://www.acts29network.org/acts-29-blog/happy-birthday -and-happy-15th-anniversary-mark-driscoll.

15. Ruth Graham, "How a Megachurch Melts Down," *Atlantic*, November 7, 2014, https://www.theatlantic.com/national/archive/2014/11/houston -mark-driscoll-megachurch-meltdown/382487.

16. Jonathan Merritt, "Mark Driscoll Makes Pacifists Fighting Mad," Religion News Service, October 24, 2013, https://religionnews.com/2013/10/24/mark-driscolls-pansy-post-outrages-christian-pacifists.

17. A whole book could be written about male Christian celebrities and their masculine leadership styles. Indeed, Kristin du Mez has written it: *Jesus and John Wayne: How White Evangelicals Corrupted a Faith and Fractured a Nation* (New York: Liveright, 2020).

18. Kate Shellnutt, "Harvest Elders Say James MacDonald Is 'Biblically Disqualified' from Ministry," *Christianity Today*, November 5, 2019, https://www.christianitytoday.com/news/2019/november/harvest-elders-say-james-macdonald-biblically-disqualified.html.

19. Bob Smietana, "Is Dave Ramsey's Empire the 'Best Place to Work in America'? Say No and You're Out," Religion News Service, January 15, 2021, https://religionnews.com/2021/01/15/dave-ramsey-is-tired-of-being-called-a-jerk-for-his-stands-on-sex-and-covid.

20. Steven Hale, "Deposition: Yes, Dave Ramsey Pulled Out a Gun in a Staff Meeting," *Nashville Scene*, November 6, 2019, https://www.nashvillescene.com/news/pithinthewind/deposition-yes-dave-ramsey-pulled-out-a-gun-in-a-staff-meeting/article_1e2f5737-7e82-53e6-a99f-817d5b189c05.html.

21. Cosper, *Rise and Fall of Mars Hill*.

22. Mark Driscoll, "The Man," Acts 29 Bootcamp, Raleigh, NC, September 20, 2007, quoted in Wendy Alsup, "Review of *Real Marriage* by Mark and Grace Driscoll," *Practical Theology for Women*, February 21, 2012, https://theologyforwomen.org/2012/02/our-review-of-real-marriage-by-mark-and-grace-driscoll.html.

23. Sarah Pulliam Bailey, "Pastors' Letter on Mark Driscoll: Step Down from All Aspects of Ministry and Leadership," Religion News Service, August 28, 2014, https://religionnews.com/2014/08/28/mars-hill-pastors-letter-mark-driscoll-step-down-ministry-leadership.

24. Roxanne Stone, "Celeb Pastor Carl Lentz, Ousted from Hillsong NYC, Confesses He Was 'Unfaithful' to His Wife," Religion News Service, November 4, 2020, https://religionnews.com/2020/11/04/carl-lentz-pastor-of-hillsong-east-coast-and-justin-bieber-terminated-for-moral-failure.

25. "Justin Bieber: In the Name of My New Father . . . ," *TMZ*, July 27, 2017, https://www.tmz.com/2017/07/27/justin-bieber-pastor-carl-lentz-father-figure.

26. Rachel DeSantis, "Hillsong Founder Says Carl Lentz Had Multiple 'Significant' Affairs in Leaked Audio: Report," *People*, December 4, 2020, https://people.com/human-interest/hillsong-founder-leaked-audio-carl-lentz-affairs-report.

27. Ruth Graham, "The Rise and Fall of Carl Lentz, the Celebrity Pastor of Hillsong Church," *New York Times*, December 5, 2020, https://www.nytimes.com/2020/12/05/us/carl-lentz-hillsong-pastor.html.

28. Fergus Hunter, Laura Chung, and Alexandra Smith, "Hillsong Pastor Brian Houston Charged for Allegedly Concealing Child Sexual Abuse by His Father," *Sydney Morning Herald*, August 5, 2021, https://www.smh.com.au /national/nsw/hillsong-pastor-brian-houston-charged-for-allegedly-conceal ing-child-sexual-abuse-by-his-father-20210805-p58g7z.html; Maura Hohman, "Hillsong Founder Brian Houston Opens Up about Church's Controversies, Ex-pastor Carl Lentz," NBC Today, May 18, 2021, https://www.today.com/news /hillsong-founder-brian-houston-breaks-silence-church-s-controversies-t218822.

29. Hannah Frishberg, "Tithe Money Funded Hillsong Pastors' Luxury Lifestyles: Former Members," *New York Post*, January 26, 2021, https:// nypost.com/2021/01/26/former-hillsong-members-detail-pastors-lavish -lifestyles.

30. Joe Pinsker, "Why So Many Americans Don't Talk about Money," *Atlantic*, March 2, 2020, https://www.theatlantic.com/family/archive/2020 /03/americans-dont-talk-about-money-taboo/607273.

31. Whitney Bauck, "Meet the Instagram Account Calling Out Celebrity Pastors for Their Expensive Sneakers," April 4, 2019, *Fashionista*, https:// fashionista.com/2019/04/celebrity-pastors-preachers-sneakers-instagram.

32. Bauck, "Meet the Instagram Account."

33. Sarah Pulliam Bailey, "Major Evangelical Nonprofits Are Trying a New Strategy with the IRS That Allows Them to Hide Their Salaries," *Washington Post*, January 17, 2020, https://www.washingtonpost.com/religion/2020/01/17 /major-evangelical-nonprofits-are-trying-new-strategy-with-irs-that-allows -them-hide-their-salaries.

34. Warren Cole Smith, "When a Church Is Not a Church," Ministry-Watch, December 19, 2019, https://ministrywatch.com/when-a-church-is-not -a-church.

35. Smith, "When a Church Is Not a Church."

36. "Seven Standards of Responsible Stewardship," Evangelical Council for Financial Accountability, https://www.ecfa.org/Content/Standards.

37. Taylor Berglund, "John Crist Cancels 2019 Tour Dates after Reports of Sexting, Harassment, Manipulation," *Charisma*, November 6, 2019, https:// www.charismanews.com/us/78703-john-crist-cancels-2019-tour-dates-after -reports-of-sexting-harassment-manipulation.

38. Berglund, "John Crist Cancels 2019 Tour Dates."

39. Lisa Respers France, "Christian Comedian John Crist Apologizes after Sexual Misconduct Allegations," CNN, November 17, 2019, https:// www.cnn.com/2019/11/07/entertainment/john-crist-sexual-misconduct-trnd /index.html.

40. Kate Shellnutt, "Comedian John Crist: 'The Biggest Hypocrite Was Me,'" *Christianity Today*, July 15, 2020, https://www.christianitytoday.com/news /2020/july/john-crist-comedian-facebook-back-online-christian-video.html.

41. Berglund, "John Crist Cancels 2019 Tour Dates."

42. Berglund, "John Crist Cancels 2019 Tour Dates."

43. Berglund, "John Crist Cancels 2019 Tour Dates."

44. "Transcript: Donald Trump's Taped Comments about Women," *New York Times*, October 8, 2016, https://www.nytimes.com/2016/10/08 /us/donald-trump-tape-transcript.html.

45. John Crist, "A message from me ☺," Facebook, July 15, 2020, https:// www.facebook.com/johnbcrist/videos/941973542950323.

46. Lynsey M. Barron and William P. Eiselstein, "Report of Independent Investigation into Sexual Misconduct of Ravi Zacharias," February 9, 2021, https://s3-us-west-2.amazonaws.com/rzimmedia.rzim.org/assets/downloads /Report-of-Investigation.pdf.

47. Barron and Eiselstein, "Report of Independent Investigation."

48. "Open Letter from the International Board of Directors of RZIM on the Investigation of Ravi Zacharias," https://rzim.org/read/rzim-updates /board-statement.html.

49. "Open Letter from the International Board of Directors."

50. French, "'You Are One Step Away.'"

51. Bob Smietana, "She Wanted to Help Ravi Zacharias Save the World but Ended Up Defending an Abuser," Religion News Service, August 13, 2021, https://religionnews.com/2021/08/13/ruth-malhorta-wanted-to-help -save-the-world-instead-she-ended-up-defending-an-abuser-raavi-zacharias -alori-anne-thompson.

52. Smietana, "She Wanted to Help Ravi Zacharias."

53. Ruth Malhotra, "Letter to RZIM Board Chairman," February 6, 2021, https:// docs.google.com/document/d/1UsmGx0KFQaSDznIpyMgXjeVGV3OD-zEK ptrrZrvoWPo/edit, quoted in French, "'You Are One Step Away.'"

54. Malhotra, "Letter to RZIM Board Chairman."

55. Malhotra, "Letter to RZIM Board Chairman."

56. ThirtyOne:Eight, "Spiritual Abuse: A Position Paper," February 2018, page 6, https://thirtyoneeight.org/media/2191/spiritual-abuse-position-state ment.pdf.

57. Malhotra, "Letter to RZIM Board Chairman."

58. Daniel Gilman, quoted in French, "'You Are One Step Away.'"

Chapter 5: Chasing Platforms

1. Jim Milliot, "Industry Sales Dipped in 2018," *Publishers Weekly*, June 28, 2019, https://www.publishersweekly.com/pw/by-topic/industry-news /bookselling/article/80592-industry-sales-dipped-in-2018.html.

2. Ben Witherington III, "The Most Dangerous Thing Luther Did," *Christian History*, October 17, 2017, https://www.christianitytoday.com/history /2017/october/most-dangerous-thing-luther-did.html.

3. Dave Roos, "7 Ways the Printing Press Changed the World," *History*, August 23, 2019, updated September 3, 2019, https://www.history.com/news /printing-press-renaissance.

4. Daniel Vaca, *Evangelicals Incorporated: Books and the Business of Religion in America* (Cambridge, MA: Harvard University Press, 2019), 13.

5. Vaca, *Evangelicals Incorporated*, 2.

6. Daniel Silliman, "The Business of Evangelical Book Publishing Is Business," *Christianity Today*, December 12, 2019, https://www.christianitytoday.com/ct/2019/december-web-only/evangelicals-incorporated-books-business-daniel-vaca.html.

7. Daniel Silliman, *Reading Evangelicals: How Christian Fiction Shaped a Culture and a Faith* (Grand Rapids: Eerdmans, 2021).

8. Ted Olsen, "HarperCollins Buys Thomas Nelson, Will Control 50% of Christian Publishing Market," *Christianity Today*, October 31, 2011, https://www.christianitytoday.com/news/2011/october/harpercollins-buys-thomas-nelson-will-control-50-of.html.

9. Vaca, *Evangelicals Incorporated*, 96.

10. Daniel J. Boorstin, *The Image: A Guide to Pseudo-Events in America* (1962; repr., New York: Knopf, 2012), 53.

11. Joshua Harris, Instagram post, July 26, 2019, https://www.instagram.com/p/B0ZBrNLH2sl/.

12. Carl R. Trueman, "Josh Harris's Message Remains the Same," *First Things*, August 12, 2021, https://www.firstthings.com/web-exclusives/2021/08/josh-harriss-message-remains-the-same.

13. Christopher Hitchens, "About Books," interview with Brian Lamb, C-SPAN, aired October 26, 1997, https://www.c-span.org/video/?94062-1/political-books.

14. Phil Cooke, "The Truth about Using Ghostwriters for Christian Books," PhilCooke.com, July 28, 2017, https://www.philcooke.com/ghostwriting.

15. Andy Crouch, "The Real Problem with Mark Driscoll's 'Citation Errors,'" *Christianity Today*, December 10, 2013, https://www.christianitytoday.com/ct/2013/december-web-only/real-problem-with-mark-driscolls-citation-errors.html.

16. Crouch, "Real Problem with Mark Driscoll's 'Citation Errors.'"

17. Jonathan Merritt, "Mars Hill Church Admits to 'Citation Errors' in Driscoll Plagiarism Controversy," Religion News Service, December 9, 2013, https://religionnews.com/2013/12/09/mars-hill-church-plagiarism-controversy-citation-errors.

18. Colleen Flaherty, "Former Liberty U Professor Denies Plagiarism Allegations," *Inside Higher Ed*, August 14, 2018, https://www.insidehighered.com/quicktakes/2018/08/14/former-liberty-u-professor-denies-plagiarism-allegations.

19. Emily Belz, "Back to the Sources," *World*, October 11, 2018, https://wng.org/articles/back-to-the-sources-1617300355.

20. Gregory A. Smith, "Giving Credit Where Credit Is Due: Avoiding Plagiarism in Christian Writing and Speaking," Liberty University Faculty Publications and Presentations, 2006, https://digitalcommons.liberty

.edu/cgi/viewcontent.cgi?referer=&httpsredir=1&article=1045&context= lib_fac_pubs.

21. Kate Bowler, *The Preacher's Wife: The Precarious Power of Evangelical Women Celebrities* (Princeton: Princeton University Press, 2019), xiii.

22. Katelyn Beaty, "Behind the Rise of Evangelical Women 'Influencers,'" *Religion and Politics*, December 10, 2019, https://religionandpolitics.org/2019 /12/10/behind-the-rise-of-evangelical-women-influencers.

23. Nick Bilton, quoted in Tom Huddleston Jr., "How Instagram Influencers Can Fake Their Way to Online Fame," CNBC, February 4, 2021, https://www .cnbc.com/2021/02/02/hbo-fake-famous-how-instagram-influencers-.html.

24. Emma Grey Ellis, "Fighting Instagram's $1.3 Billion Problem—Fake Followers," *Wired*, September 10, 2019, https://www.wired.com/story /instagram-fake-followers.

25. Trueman, "Josh Harris's Message Remains the Same."

26. Warren Throckmorton, "Thomas Nelson Contract: Mark Driscoll's Real Marriage Advance Was $400,000," *Warren Throckmorton* (blog), January 5, 2016, https://www.wthrockmorton.com/2016/01/05/thomas-nelson -contract-mark-driscolls-real-marriage-advance-was-400000.

27. Warren Throckmorton, "How the Religious Right Scams Its Way onto the *New York Times* Bestseller List," *Daily Beast*, November 16, 2014, https://www.thedailybeast.com/how-the-religious-right-scams-its-way-onto -the-new-york-times-bestseller-list.

28. Warren Cole Smith, "Unreal Sales for Driscoll's *Real Marriage*," *World*, March 5, 2014, https://wng.org/sift/unreal-sales-for-driscolls-real -marriage-1617422429.

29. Dwight Baker, quoted in Ken Walker, "Is Buying Your Way onto the Bestseller List Wrong?," *Christianity Today*, January 20, 2015, https:// www.christianitytoday.com/ct/2015/januaryfebruary/buying-bestsellers -resultsource.html.

30. Sarah Nicolas, "A History of Buying Books onto the Bestseller List," *Book Riot*, January 6, 2020, https://bookriot.com/buying-books-onto-the -bestseller-list.

31. Vanessa Barthelmes, "Jesus Cleanses the Temple: What Does It Mean for You?," JadoreVaness.com, January 6, 2020, https://www.jadorevanessa .com/jesus-cleanses-the-temple-what-does-it-mean-for-you.

Chapter 6: Creating Persona

1. Bruce Weber, "Philip Seymour Hoffman, Actor of Depth, Dies at 46," *New York Times*, February 2, 2014, https://www.nytimes.com/2014/02/03 /movies/philip-seymour-hoffman-actor-dies-at-46.html.

2. David Browne, "Philip Seymour Hoffman's Last Days," *Rolling Stone*, July 25, 2014, https://www.rollingstone.com/movies/movie-news/philip -seymour-hoffmans-last-days-77972.

3. Vinson Cunningham, "The Impenetrable Genius of Prince," *New Yorker*, April 25, 2016, https://www.newyorker.com/magazine/2016/05/02/the-impenetrable-genius-of-prince.

4. Amy Forliti, "Investigation Says Prince Was Isolated, Addicted and in Pain," Associated Press, April 20, 2018, https://apnews.com/article/music-north-america-us-news-ap-top-news-prince-94806d16569541d98032ce2b2f82aa6a.

5. Jennifer Michael Hecht, "How the Media Covers Celebrity Suicides Can Have Life-or-Death Consequences," *Vox*, June 8, 2018, https://www.vox.com/first-person/2018/5/5/17319632/anthony-bourdain-kate-spade-cause-of-death-suicide-celebrities-reporting.

6. Cydney Henderson, "Daniel Radcliffe Says He Used Alcohol to Manage the Unmagical Bits of 'Harry Potter' Fame," *USA Today*, February 20, 2019, https://www.usatoday.com/story/life/people/2019/02/20/daniel-radcliffe-turned-alcohol-cope-harry-potter-fame/2931072002.

7. Maria Cavassuto, "Lady Gaga: Fame Is the Most Isolating Thing in the World," *Variety*, June 3, 2016, https://variety.com/2016/tv/news/lady-gaga-fame-isolation-jamie-lee-curtis-1201787973.

8. Molly Lambert, "I Feel like a Zoo Animal: The Ballad of Justin Bieber," *MTV News*, May 11, 2016, https://www.mtv.com/news/2879694/justin-bieber-feel-like-zoo-animal.

9. Donna Rockwell and David C. Giles, "Being a Celebrity: A Phenomenology of Fame," *Journal of Phenomenological Psychology* 40 (2009): 178–210.

10. Rockwell and Giles, "Being a Celebrity."

11. Hannah Arendt, "Sonning Prize," speech, Copenhagen, Denmark, April 18, 1975 (Washington, DC: Hannah Arendt Papers at the Library of Congress), 12–13, quoted in Mike Cosper, *Recapturing the Wonder: Transcendent Faith in a Disenchanted World* (Downers Grove, IL: InterVarsity, 2017), 82.

12. Arendt, "Sonning Prize," quoted in Cosper, *Recapturing the Wonder*, 82.

13. Chuck DeGroat, phone interview with the author, October 4, 2021.

14. Chuck DeGroat, *When Narcissism Comes to Church: Healing Your Community from Emotional and Spiritual Abuse* (Downers Grove, IL: InterVarsity, 2020).

15. Paroma Mitra and Dimy Fluyau, "Narcissistic Personality Disorder," National Center for Biotechnology Information, May 18, 2021, https://www.ncbi.nlm.nih.gov/books/NBK556001.

16. Chuck DeGroat, "Finding Narcissism in Church," *Banner*, December 28, 2020, https://www.thebanner.org/features/2020/12/finding-narcissism-in-church.

17. Darrell Puls, quoted in Matthew Heisler, "Power and Authority in Spiritual Abuse," *MatthewHeisler.com*, May 12, 2020, updated June 26, 2020, https://www.matthewheisler.com/post/power-and-authority-part-3-of-the-spiritual-abuse-series.

18. Robert Enroth, quoted in Scot McKnight, "Help! My Pastor Is a Narcissist," *Jesus Creed* (blog), Christianity Today blog forum, August 10, 2020, https://www.christianitytoday.com/scot-mcknight/2020/august/help -my-pastor-is-narcissist.html.

19. DeGroat, *When Narcissism Comes to Church*, 23.

20. DeGroat, *When Narcissism Comes to Church*, 23.

21. C. S. Lewis, *Mere Christianity* (1952; repr., New York: HarperCollins, 2001), 86.

22. Rich Villodas, "The Celebrity Pastor Problem Is Every Church's Struggle," *Christianity Today*, December 8, 2020, https://www.christianitytoday .com/pastors/2020/december-web-exclusives/celebrity-pastor-entitlement -church-culture-humility.html.

23. Lisa Cannon Green, "Despite Stresses, Few Pastors Give Up on Ministry," LifeWay Research, September 1, 2015, https://lifewayresearch.com/2015 /09/01/despite-stresses-few-pastors-give-up-on-ministry.

24. Carey Nieuwhof, "29 Percent of Pastors Want to Quit: How to Keep Going When You've Lost Confidence in Yourself," updated September 14, 2021, https://careynieuwhof.com/29-of-pastors-want-to-quit-how-to-keep -going-when-youve-lost-confidence-in-yourself.

25. LifeWay Research, "Pastors Feel Privileged and Positive, Though Discouragement Can Come," LifeWay Research, October 5, 2011, https:// lifewayresearch.com/2011/10/05/pastors-feel-privileged-and-positive-though -discouragement-can-come.

26. Henri Nouwen, *In the Name of Jesus: Reflections on Christian Leadership* (London: Darton, Longman and Todd, 1989), 9.

27. Kayleigh Donaldson, "The Personal, Private, and Parasocial of John Mulaney," *Pajiba*, May 18, 2021, https://www.pajiba.com/celebrities_are _better_than_you/the-personal-private-and-parasocial-of-john-mulaney.php.

28. Donald Horton and R. Richard Wohl, "Mass Communication and Para-social Interaction: Observations on Intimacy at a Distance," *Psychiatry* 19, no. 3 (1956): 215.

29. Horton and Wohl, "Mass Communication and Para-social Interaction," quoted in *Mass Communication and American Social Thought: Key Texts, 1919–1968*, ed. John Durham Peters and Peter Simonson (Lanham, MD: Rowman & Littlefield, 2004), 375.

30. Horton and Wohl, "Mass Communication and Para-social Interaction," quoted in Peters and Simonson, *Mass Communication and American Social Thought*, 375.

31. Griffin Wynne, "Parasocial Relationships with Celebrities Aren't Necessarily a Bad Thing," *Bustle*, September 14, 2021, https://www.bustle.com /wellness/why-parasocial-relationships-not-all-bad.

32. Gary Laderman, *Sacred Matters: Celebrity Worship, Sexual Ecstasies, the Living Dead, and Other Signs of Religious Life in the United States* (New York: New Press, 2009), 87.

Chapter 7: Seeking Brand Ambassadors

1. Dorian Lynskey, "Natural Born Show-Off," *Guardian*, August 4, 2005, https://www.theguardian.com/music/2005/aug/05/kanyewest.

2. Carrie Battan, "Kanye West's True Salvation on 'Jesus Is King,'" *New Yorker*, October 27, 2019, https://www.newyorker.com/culture/cultural -comment/kanye-wests-true-salvation-on-jesus-is-king.

3. Trevin Wax, "Kanye West, Justin Bieber, and What to Make of Celebrity Conversions," The Gospel Coalition, September 23, 2019, https://www .thegospelcoalition.org/blogs/trevin-wax/kanye-west-justin-bieber-make -celebrity-conversions.

4. Lindsay Elizabeth, "Kanye West: 'It's My Job to Let People Know What Jesus Has Done for Me,'" *Christian Broadcasting Network*, October 28, 2019, https://www1.cbn.com/cbnnews/entertainment/2019/october/kanye-west-its -my-job-to-let-people-know-what-jesus-has-done-for-me.

5. Andrew Trendell, "Watch Kanye West's Sunday Service Cover Nirvana Classics with a Christian Spin," *NME*, July 29, 2019, https://www.nme .com/news/music/watch-kanye-wests-sunday-service-cover-nirvana-classics -christian-spin-2533233.

6. Robert Hilburn and *Los Angeles Times*, "Bob Dylan's Song of Salvation," *Washington Post*, November 24, 1980, https://www.washingtonpost .com/archive/lifestyle/1980/11/24/bob-dylans-song-of-salvation/1fba5ce3 -e6fa-40dc-8a17-a384bb537643.

7. Randall J. Stephens, *The Devil's Music: How Christians Inspired, Condemned, and Embraced Rock 'N' Roll* (Cambridge, MA: Harvard University Press, 2018), 196.

8. Bob Dylan, quoted in David W. Stowe, *No Sympathy for the Devil: Christian Pop Music and the Transformation of American Evangelicalism* (Chapel Hill: University of North Carolina Press, 2011), 230.

9. Michael Simmons, quoted in Lesli White, "The Incredible Faith of Bob Dylan," Beliefnet, updated June 12, 2020, https://www.beliefnet.com /entertainment/music/the-incredible-faith-of-bob-dylan.aspx.

10. White, "Incredible Faith of Bob Dylan."

11. Jerry Falwell, quoted in Doug Banwart, "Jerry Falwell, the Rise of the Moral Majority, and the 1980 Election," *Western Illinois Historical Review* 5 (Spring 2013): 1, http://www.wiu.edu/cas/history/wihr/pdfs/Banwart -MoralMajorityVol5.pdf.

12. Hilburn and *Los Angeles Times*, "Bob Dylan's Song of Salvation."

13. Aaron E. Sanchez, "Bob Dylan's Overlooked Christian Music," *Sojourners*, September 3, 2019, https://sojo.net/articles/bob-dylans-overlooked -christian-music.

14. Stan Guthrie, "Bob Dylan: Is He or Isn't He?," The Gospel Coalition, August 14, 2017, https://www.thegospelcoalition.org/reviews/bob-dylan -a-spiritual-life.

15. Bill Dwyer was reportedly Dylan's Bible class teacher at Vineyard Christian Fellowship Church. Larry Myers and Paul Emond were two Vineyard pastors sent to Dylan's home to pray with him. Composer Al Kasha also claims to have prayed the Sinner's Prayer with Dylan.

16. Kara Bettis, "Master's Seminary Grad Takes Kanye's Crowds to Church," *Christianity Today*, October 2, 2019, https://www.christianity today.com/ct/2019/october-web-only/masters-seminary-grad-takes-kanyes -crowds-to-church.html.

17. John Stott, *The Message of the Sermon on the Mount* (Downers Grove, IL: InterVarsity, 2020), 35.

18. Alan Noble, "The Evangelical Persecution Complex," *Atlantic*, August 4, 2014, https://www.theatlantic.com/national/archive/2014/08/the-evangeli cal-persecution-complex/375506.

19. Noble, "Evangelical Persecution Complex."

20. Stott, *Message of the Sermon on the Mount*, 35.

21. Noble, "Evangelical Persecution Complex."

22. Allie Jones, "A Guide to the Evangelical Celebrities and Pastors Dominating Hollywood," *The Cut*, August 6, 2018, https://www.thecut.com/2018 /08/justin-bieber-hailey-baldwin-hillsong-evangelicals-hollywood.html.

23. Brittany Raymer, "Kanye West's Gospel Album Includes an Ode to Chick-fil-A's Lemonade and a Distinctly Christian Message," *Daily Citizen*, October 25, 2019, https://dailycitizen.focusonthefamily.com/kanye-wests -gospel-album-includes-an-ode-to-chick-fil-as-lemonade-and-a-distinctly -christian-message.

24. Madeline Berg, "Here's How Much Money Is at Stake in a Kim Kardashian–Kanye West Divorce," *Forbes*, January 6, 2021, https://www.forbes .com/sites/maddieberg/2021/01/06/heres-how-much-money-is-at-stake-in -a-kim-kardashian-kanye-west-divorce.

25. Gil Kaufman, "Kanye West Says His $68 Million Tax Refund Was Divinely Inspired—So We Asked a CPA if That's a Thing," *Billboard*, October 30, 2019, https://www.billboard.com/articles/columns/hip-hop/8541528 /kanye-west-tax-refund-cpa-interview.

26. Wax, "Kanye West, Justin Bieber, and What to Make of Celebrity Conversions."

27. Brett McCracken, "Hipster Faith," *Christianity Today*, September 3, 2010, https://www.christianitytoday.com/ct/2010/september/9.24.html.

28. Laura Turner, "The Rise of the Star-Studded, Instagram-Friendly Evangelical Church," *Vox*, February 6, 2019, https://www.vox.com/culture /2019/2/6/18205355/church-chris-pratt-justin-bieber-zoe-hillsong.

29. Taffy Brodesser-Akner, "Inside Hillsong, the Church of Choice for Justin Bieber and Kevin Durant," *GQ*, December 17, 2015, https://www.gq .com/story/inside-hillsong-church-of-justin-bieber-kevin-durant.

30. Gabrielle Chung, "Justin Bieber Shares Photos from His Joint Baptism with Wife Hailey Baldwin: 'Trust in Jesus,'" *People*, August 5, 2020,

https://people.com/music/justin-bieber-shares-photos-from-joint-baptism-with-hailey-baldwin.

31. Justin Bieber, "Wowzers," Instagram, January 6, 2018, https://www.instagram.com/p/BdoOL5Gjip4.

32. Rania Aniftos, "Kanye West Defends Comments That Slavery Was a Choice: 'We Can't Be Mentally Imprisoned for Another 400 Years,'" *Billboard*, May 1, 2018, https://www.billboard.com/articles/news/8430171/kanye-west-defends-tmz-comments-slavery-was-a-choice.

33. Emily Kirkpatrick, "More Hillsong Pastors Resign as Justin Bieber Confirms He's Left the Church," *Vanity Fair*, January 5, 2021, https://www.vanityfair.com/style/2021/01/justin-bieber-not-part-of-hillsong-church-carl-lentz-scandal-pastors-resign.

34. Zach Baron, "The Redemption of Justin Bieber," *GQ*, April 13, 2021, https://www.gq.com/story/justin-bieber-cover-profile-may-2021.

35. Turner, "Rise of the Star-Studded, Instagram-Friendly Evangelical Church."

Chapter 8: The Obscure Messiah and Ordinary Faithfulness

1. C. S. Lewis, *Mere Christianity* (1952; repr., New York: Simon & Schuster, 1996), 171.

2. Conrad Hackett and David McClendon, "Christians Remain World's Largest Religious Group, but They Are Declining in Europe," Pew Research Center, April 5, 2017, https://www.pewresearch.org/fact-tank/2017/04/05/christians-remain-worlds-largest-religious-group-but-they-are-declining-in-europe.

3. Jaroslav Pelikan, *Jesus through the Centuries: His Place in the History of Culture* (New Haven: Yale University Press, 1985), 1.

4. Dallas Willard, *The Divine Conspiracy: Rediscovering Our Hidden Life in God* (New York: HarperCollins, 2009), 11–12.

5. Willard, *Divine Conspiracy*, 16.

6. Andy Crouch, "It's Time to Reckon with Celebrity Power," The Gospel Coalition, March 24, 2018, https://www.thegospelcoalition.org/article/time-reckon-celebrity-power.

7. Henri Nouwen, *In the Name of Jesus: Reflections on Christian Leadership* (London: Darton, Longman and Todd, 1989), 76–77.

8. Eugene Peterson, *The Jesus Way: A Conversation on the Ways That Jesus Is the Way* (Grand Rapids: Eerdmans, 2007), 33.

9. Peterson, *Jesus Way*, 35.

10. Crouch, "It's Time to Reckon with Celebrity Power."

11. Andy Crouch, interview with the author, October 27, 2021.

12. George Eliot, *Middlemarch: A Study in Provincial Life* (New York: Penguin Classics, 1994), 838.